THE

SOCIAL GOSPEL RE-EXAMINED

THE
SOCIAL GOSPEL
RE-EXAMINED

by

F. ERNEST JOHNSON

HARPER & BROTHERS PUBLISHERS
NEW YORK AND LONDON

The Rauschenbusch Lectureship Foundation of the Colgate-Rochester Divinity School, Rochester, New York

THE RAUSCHENBUSCH FOUNDATION WAS ESTABLISHED IN March 1929 at the Colgate-Rochester Divinity School in memory of the late Walter Rauschenbusch, illustrious exponent of social Christianity and, from 1902 to 1918, professor of church history in the Rochester Theological Seminary, to which institution the Colgate-Rochester Divinity School is successor.

The movement for the establishment of this foundation was initiated by a gift of ten thousand dollars from Mrs. Edmund Lyon, of Rochester, New York, conditioned upon the raising of twenty-five thousand dollars from other sources. An amount somewhat in excess of that sum was secured through the generous gifts of citizens of Rochester, alumni of the Rochester Theological Seminary, and others.

The general field of the lectureship is that of Christianity in its social expression and application. A series of lectures upon this foundation is to be given annually during the week of the Spring Convocation at the Colgate-Rochester Divinity School, these lectures to be published in book form and known as the Rauschenbusch Lectures.

Publications on
The Rauschenbusch Lectureship Foundation

THE MORAL CRISIS IN CHRISTIANITY
Justin Wroe Nixon

THE SOCIAL GOSPEL AND THE CHRISTIAN CULTUS
Charles Clayton Morrison

THE SOCIAL TRIUMPH OF THE ANCIENT CHURCH
Shirley Jackson Case

AN INTERPRETATION OF CHRISTIAN ETHICS
Reinhold Niebuhr

CHURCH AND STATE IN THE MODERN WORLD
Henry Pitney Van Dusen, et al.

THIS NATION UNDER GOD
Arthur Erastus Holt

THE SOCIAL GOSPEL RE-EXAMINED
F. Ernest Johnson

CONTENTS

PREFACE

SINCE the Rauschenbusch Lectures for 1939 were delivered much has happened to the world. In the process of elaborating them into book form the main thesis and the general course of the argument have been preserved, but at a number of points the drama of recent world events is reflected in the discussion. In particular, the treatment of the Christian testimony concerning war has been extended.

The purpose of the lectures has been to consider the net result of the impact of recent theological changes upon what has been known in America as the social gospel; to offer suggestions for a restatement of the general position which has gone by that name; and to clarify some of the major ethical problems of our time. I have written both as a critic of "liberal social Christianity" and as one who nevertheless believes that there is something authentic in what may be called the Rauschenbusch tradition which it is all-important to preserve. The term "social gospel" is retained advisedly, though with a full appreciation of the freight of misunderstanding that it carries. Until what it has stood for has been fairly appraised I do not care to have its standard hauled down.

If this book contributes to a synthesis of conflicting points of view—substituting appreciative evaluation for mere polemics—and if it assists in relating tenable beliefs to social action in terms of a Christian strategy for our day, it will have served its purpose.

F. E. J.

New York, July 1, 1940

THE

SOCIAL GOSPEL RE-EXAMINED

INTRODUCTION

FOR many years the struggle to gain recognition in America for an authoritative Christian social ethic was carried on upon two fronts, the one religious, in the strict sense of the word, the other economic. Roughly, it may be said that the religious opposition to what has come to be called the "social gospel" came from conservative clergy who feared that enthusiasm for a Christian social ethic was doing violence to the historic concern of Christianity for the redemption of the individual—in other words, that the evangelical message was being diluted. The most vigorous opposition came from the "fundamentalist" wing of Protestantism. Broadly speaking, within evangelical Christianity, the theological reconstructionists have been the social liberals. Supporting the conservative clergy in their opposition to the growing social emphasis within the churches were the economic conservatives among the laity, with whom that movement has always been suspect. Their attitude has been determined not alone by self-interest—from which none of us is free—but by an honest conviction that the liberal clergy were

[1]

getting away beyond their depth in economics and politics.

These generalizations are, of course, only approximately accurate; many exceptions may be cited. On the whole, however, it is doubtful if many close observers of the religious scene in America during the past thirty years will question their essential correctness. The two groups referred to, clerical and lay, have had this in common: both of them, though for different reasons, have insisted that the socialization of the Christian message is false to its historic character.

Today the situation has changed in an important way. Conservative lay opposition to the social gospel continues on the old lines, but the theological front has re-formed. It is now led by preachers, teachers and writers who are at opposite poles from the fundamentalists, who eschew biblical literalism, who would scorn to oppose the teaching of evolutionary science in the schools, and whose interpretation of historic Christian doctrine involves the use of a frankly avowed mythology. Furthermore, many of them are radical in their political and economic views. It is this group that has been forcing the liberal wing of Protestantism to re-examine its assumptions and restate its case. The social gospel movement is criticized on the ground that it is theologically shallow, that it has missed the real meaning of the Kingdom of God in relation to history; that it is "humanistic" and lacking in recognition of the supernatural factors in redemption; that it has glorified the immanence of God at the expense of his "otherness"; that it is hopelessly romantic in its conception of human nature; that it has substituted for divine architecture the work of men's hands. While it would be quite false to attribute identical views to all those who bring forward such criticisms, and while labels are always misleading, it may be said that a fairly well-defined school of writers and teachers has appeared which is held together by a transcendentalist emphasis and by an aversion for the developmental, immanentist emphasis which has characterized the social gospel. The entire trend represented by this school I shall call the neo-(new) orthodoxy. Perhaps neo-Protestantism would be a more accurate term but the other is more conveniently descriptive. The challenge of these writers and teachers is not to be taken lightly. Least of all should it be made the subject of merely defensive polemics. It is to be feared that many of us who have been associated with the pursuit of what we considered Christian social objectives have, when confronted by this movement, erred on the side of defensive argument and have been slow in appreciating the significance and the importance of the current orthodox reaction. Indeed, I hope to show that a tenable view of the function of theology furnishes no small basis for a reconciliation between this movement and liberal social Christianity.

Let it be understood at the outset that this is going to be a theological discussion only in a limited sense. No attempt will be made at a systematic statement of Christian social philosophy. That is a task for an academic theologian, which the author is not. Moreover, the work in hand is not of that kind; its purpose is rather to indicate some basic elements of a Christian social ethic that is both authentically derived and relevant to the contemporary situation in America. For it can scarcely be denied that the effort to build a social ethic within liberal Christianity in America has rested on a scant foundation in theology.

It is a valid criticism of this liberal social Christianity that its philosophy, its ideals and its programs as commonly stated have little distinctive character in terms of Christian postulates. Many of the social pronouncements of church bodies in this country might have been made by any high-minded group of educators or social workers claiming nothing other than a secular sanction. This does not invalidate them as declarations of ideals or of purposes but it leaves them unattached to the driving power of a religious tradition and a religious cultus, of which a religious community, as such, is custodian. If there is anything distinctive about Christianity that quality should be found in all

[4]

its formulations of purpose and in all its programs. This would seem to be the principal meaning of the somewhat ambiguous slogan, "Let the Church be the Church."

Consider, for example, the formula commonly taken to epitomize a liberal Christian faith: the fatherhood of God and the brotherhood of man. These are undoubtedly vital concepts and fraught with great historic significance. As such they are a part of the intellectual and ethical tradition of Christianity. Yet they are not distinctive of Christianity. The first is more correctly characterized as a part of the Hebraic-Christian tradition than as specifically Christian, although Christians believe that the ministry of Jesus greatly enriched the idea of the divine fatherhood. The second of these two concepts can be as authentically derived from the philosophy of the Enlightenment elaborated in the eighteenth century as from specifically religious sources. I say "specifically" because it would be futile, as well as misleading, to try to isolate the religious from the secular in the development of our culture. Even the most secular humanitarianism owes a debt, often unacknowledged, to the Christian religion. This fact is increasingly recognized as the seriousness of the world-wide crisis of democracy becomes apparent.

But this very diffusion of ethical ideas in which historic Christianity has had so large a part tends to blur the boundary between the Christian community and the secular community. It forces the Church to re-examine its own testimony and the quality of its corporate life in order to discover and reaffirm the distinctive elements in its teaching and in the experience of its members. If it should appear that its message is no longer anything more than what the average enlightened and conscientious person believes, there would seem to be little reason for its continuance as a distinct and self-conscious institution. If it should find itself piecing together a social ethic out of the intellectual and moral climate of American life, then Christianity, insofar as the Church represents it, would indeed be outmoded. For a religious system can be potent in a sustained and permanent way only by bringing to bear upon contemporary life some distinctive testimony, which is the vital possession of a community of believers. Unless the central beliefs that make Christianity a unitary religion can be given authentic expression in terms of social attitudes and social action it is idle to talk of a Christian ethic. Because of the vagueness of its social teaching Protestantism is in a precarious position today.

It is customary to refer the lack of a vigorous impact by Protestant Christianity upon contemporary life to its divided condition. In part, this is doubtless correct. The urge toward an ecumenical Christianity that will give the churches a larger measure of unity rests on a genuine insight into religious needs. But this is not the heart of the matter under consideration here. Not the absence of common consensus nor the lack of central authority accounts for the seeming irrelevance of the Church. The great evangelical revivals were conducted without Protestant unity. The enormous growth of church membership in this country from very meager beginnings in the Colonial period was accomplished by a divided Church. These achievements were possible because the Church had a distinctive and recognizable testimony which was relevant to the felt needs of the times. Today the felt needs of men and women are in much larger part social and ethical than in the early years. The lessening of millennial expectation, the growing interest in this present world as a theater of moral action, and the sharpening of political, social and economic conflict make heavy demands upon the Church for spiritual guidance. And the answering voice is indecisive and unheartening. The evangelical tradition does not supply as clear answers to the new questions as it did to the old.

Much attention was attracted to this unmet need on the part of the laity by an editorial that appeared a few months ago in a magazine that circulates among business men. The writer complained of the prevailing lack of ethical sanctions to which the layman can have recourse, and then declared: "The way out is the sound of a voice, not our voice, but a voice coming from something not ourselves, in the existence of which we cannot disbelieve. It is the earthly task of the pastors to hear this voice, to cause us to hear it, and to tell us what it says. If they cannot hear it, or if they fail to tell us, we, as laymen, are utterly lost. Without it we are no more capable of saving the world than we were capable of creating it in the first place."[1]

It would be missing the point to push such a complaint aside on the ground that it is merely a demand for authority and, as such, an evidence of spiritual nostalgia for a past authoritarian age. What people need as they face necessary decisions of great import in political, social and economic life is some trustworthy guidance flowing from the corporate experience of a spiritual community in which they have been nurtured. We have failed them. On the one hand we have talked about the brotherhood of man and the immeasurable worth of personality, which serious-minded people already subscribe to, at least in principle, outside the Church as well as within it. On the other hand, when we have attempted to be specific we have elaborated programs of action in controversial fields

[1] *Fortune,* January, 1940.

which represent in large part practical judgments formulated by groups of liberal clergymen, to which the laity have not given more than perfunctory and halfhearted allegiance. The task of deriving ethical mandates directly and irresistibly from Christian assumptions about man's relation to God, about sin and redemption, about love and sacrifice, about the Church, and implementing these mandates in the corporate life of a Christian community—this task we have not done in any effective way.

Now one reason for this crisis in Protestant social ethics is of course the resistance offered by middle-class society, from which the Protestant churches so largely draw their membership, to an ethical discipline in political and economic relationships. In a more individualistc age the evangelical tradition was congenial to the middle-class mind. As ethical problems become more and more social in character, bringing to the fore the prophetic elements in that tradition, resistance to its authority grows. But this fact only accentuates the Church's responsibility in the ethical realm. Can Christianity be made irresistibly relevant to crucial social problems of our time without impairing the freedom of the laity, so dear to Protestantism, to formulate their own practical ethical judgments? I believe that it can; that an effective Christian social ethic can be derived from that body of authentic

Christian teaching which Christians as such are bound to recognize, one which will stand the test of our knowledge about human nature and human affairs.

Underlying the argument of these lectures is the conviction that a sustained dynamic for ethical action is furnished only by a religious faith and that such a faith is effectively nourished only by the corporate life of a disciplined community. In noncritical periods of history religion tends to become culturally diffused and to find characteristic expression in "ideals" which have found comparatively universal recognition. This is the normal way in which religion influences cultural development. But in critical periods faith in the validity of ideals is, so to speak, forced back upon itself. Its affirmations have to be validated. For example, in the "roaring twenties" humanitarian ideals were quoted high. We were supposedly well on our way to the abolition of poverty, and even of war. Looking back we call it a materialistic decade, but this is a superficial characterization. Moral good will was not lacking. The "humane tradition" had not been discarded. But there was little recognition of the basic conflict between the forces operating in society and the lofty ideals which were everywhere proclaimed. Ethical realism was lacking.

The eclipse of the social hope which has been approaching totality during the decade just ended has a profoundly spiritual aspect. To be sure, one is disposed to look with some suspicion on the tendency to link up religion with the effort to recover prosperity. And suspicion turns to disapprobation when religious sanctions are invoked to bolster up a social order that needs more than tinkering to make it sound. A radio address a few months ago, sponsoring a movement for the revival of religious interest, boldly presented Christianity as a political fire escape. "Certainly," said the speaker, "we should carry the fight straight through, for let me tell you these new, selfish, plausible, materialistic doctrines lead straight to the confiscation of private wealth and property—the foundation of our business world, the fabric of our American civilization.

"Not only is this poison," he continued, "creeping into your homes; it is striking at the very roots of your livelihood. For every one of you who directly or indirectly controls securities, bank accounts, insurance policies—everyone of you who is in business, as I said before—is going to suffer the moment religion retires permanently from the business world, and Communism, Nazism, Fascism or Socialism takes its place." Surely nothing could be cruder than this.

Yet the layman's recourse to religion is in no small part an authentic call for adequate sanctions. The motives and methods upon which men have relied seem to have been found wanting, and the result is disillusionment. A healthy flow of hormones from the duct-less glands into a person's system may sustain a high degree of optimism, but it will not sustain his essential humanity—his assurance of *meanings* and his devotion to absorbing ends—at a time when the raw facts of life "shriek against his creed." And religion is directly associated with the critical phases of human experience. It has always been so, even in the primitive and relatively nonprophetic religions. In Christianity it is conspicuously so. The entire impact of the teachings of Jesus upon human life is a critical impact, a matter of *crisis*. Christianity becomes relevant in times of critical encounter between ideals and realities.

Thus the rhythm of social existence tends for long periods to subordinate religion to the prevailing culture and then to bring religion into sharp encounter with that culture. We are now in one of the latter periods, and this is why so much is heard today about the need of theology—and of realism in theology.

But unless historical development is to be entirely disregarded a *recovery* of theology can never be equivalent to a *return* to theology. Traditionalism must always be in some measure combated if history is to be accorded any real significance—that is to say, if anything new really happens. The very continuity of tradition means that there is an on-going concern, an abiding value to be conserved, but no less important is the reconstructive process which results from the fact that emergent needs continually challenge old concepts and formulas. The theological task of our time is to find an adequate expression for meanings that inhere in human life as such and that are timeless in their nature, in terms that will be relevant to the facts of our temporal existence. Basic to my entire argument is the conviction that no theological formulation seriously put forward and conscientiously defended can be regarded as merely "wrong." Nor can a contrary position be regarded as merely "right." Beliefs always *connote* more than they *denote*. They are directly related to felt needs in human lives. The dominance of emergent needs is the key to changing creeds. This theme is heavily stressed throughout this little book. If there were no defects in the assumptions and attitudes of liberal Christianity honest and able religious thinkers would not at this moment be persistently attacking them. But by the same token a quick retreat from a social faith that has given religious satisfaction to vast numbers of Christians who were inspired by Walter Rauschenbusch, Josiah Strong, Graham Taylor and a host of their interpreters would do violence to our religious heritage.

In a word, we must find a satisfying answer to the kind of question which, Dr. Lynn Harold Hough has reminded us, many young ministers are asking. Describing his experience on the National Preaching Mission he says: "A minister seven or eight years out of theological school would come to the leader of the seminar and would say, 'I want to talk to you about this matter of Christianity and society.' Then he would go on: 'I graduated from theological school in 1930. My school was ——' (Here he would mention any one of a half dozen of the leading theological schools of the country.) He would continue: 'I graduated just when my seminary was at the peak of its social passion. I have been preaching seven years.' Then he would stop suddenly. 'Don't get me wrong. I still believe in all the things I believed when I graduated. But'—and here he would pause rather wistfully—'strange as it is for me to say it, I must admit that the message about society is not enough. Somehow my preaching is getting thin. I feel it and I know very well that my congregations feel it. I want to find a way in which I can maintain all this enthusiasm for a better society and yet possess something which I feel that now I do not have, something which will give energy and power to my preaching.' I say that this happened in city after city."[2]

In the discussion that follows the utterances of current neo-orthodox writers will be drawn upon again and again to show that there is no necessary incon-

[2] *Free Men,* copyright 1939. Reprinted by permission of The Abingdon Press, pp. 78-79.

gruity between what has been called the social gospel
and the basic concerns of traditional Christianity; that,
on the contrary, a vigorous social ethic is vital to orthodoxy, while our liberal social Christianity needs to
rediscover its roots in the historic Christian faith.

Chapter I

THE USES OF THEOLOGY

NOTHING could be more futile than theological controversy based on allegiance to ideas held aloof from a context of experience. No great teacher has built up and maintained a following solely by means of superior intellectual architecture. Great beliefs are those that mediate great experience. It has been well said that the test of any theological belief is the effect it produces upon the person who holds it. This means that doctrine is not self-validating. It gets its validation in ethical experience. Of intellectual formulations as of men it may be said, "By their fruits ye shall know them."

Another way of putting it is that the pursuit of truth is a concomitant of purposeful living. There is an active factor in knowing. In a very true sense knowing is creative. The object of knowledge is never something static, existing "out there." Truth itself is apprehended only through an active process by which it is given relevance to things that the knower is concerned about. It is the realization of this fact that has caused education to undergo so great a transformation in recent years. It was found that any amount of effort to educate pupils simply by confronting them with statements of fact or formulas of "truth" was abortive until facts and formulas were given a context of experience. Everybody knows what it is to "come alive" quite suddenly to something long theoretically accepted, but up to that time indifferently regarded. Things take on a glow of meaning when they pass from the conceptual realm into active experience. The pursuit of truth is not an occupation *prior* to experience. We do not first "learn about" and then "learn." Do, then know, is the order that Jesus himself prescribed. Concepts are instrumental to purposes. Doctrines must be validated in living—in the experience of the individual, corrected by the experience of men in fellowship, in community.

This relevance of doctrine—in theology, psychology, economics or anything else—to personal need and intention is strikingly illustrated by the Calvinistic dogma of predestination. Of that forbidding doctrine even Milton said that though he be sent to hell for rejecting it he never would believe it. Yet it was an authentic expression of a religious mood growing out of a felt need for an unambiguous affirmation of the sovereignty of God and the divine origin of grace.

So urgent was that need that the corollary of infant damnation was accepted in order that the main proposition might stand. When the developing evangelical tradition made divine mercy and goodness a more fundamental theological requirement than divine sovereignty the earlier preoccupation with foreordination of man to eternal life or death gave way to other theological emphases.

The Apostles' Creed itself presents an anomaly which can be explained only by reference to this principle of utility. Why, in so brief a summary of our faith, should so many words be given to the physical aspects of Jesus' life and death: conceived, born, suffered, crucified, dead, buried, rose from the dead! When other important articles of the faith are omitted why so much attention to these physical elements? The answer is not far to seek. That creed seems to have had a very definite pragmatic purpose—to exclude the Docetic heretics who denied the Incarnation. (The great heresy then was not the denial that Jesus was divine but the denial that the eternal Logos was human!) The significance of the Creed in our modern worship is not that it summarizes our faith—it never did that—but rather that it mediates a sense of solidarity in faith and action with a historic Christian community.

The theology of Kierkegaard, himself one of the

sources of the new orthodoxy, furnishes an instructive modern example of the point I am emphasizing. He was an artist in paradoxes and was wont to make affirmations which logically contradicted each other. They could be true only in a "dialectical" sense, that is to say, in the sense that opposites coexist and interpenetrate. Professor H. R. Mackintosh comments thus on Kierkegaard's paradoxes: "He was well aware of the dangers involved in a Christology so paradoxical—the danger, above all, that the Incarnation might come to be thought not astonishing merely, but impossible, and the Fatherhood of God thus be lost all over again—and against these dangers he sought to guard himself. But he was resolved to make two points clear. First, by the irrationality of the Gospel he means something which evokes a sudden glory in the mind, a specific sense of wonder. To put it so, the Person of Jesus is not absurd or irrational for God, but only for us. . . . And secondly, by insisting on irrational paradox he seeks to bring out the indubitable element of provocativeness in the Gospel—what the New Testament calls the *offence* of the Cross."[1]

Thus the formulation of a creed becomes the conscious creation of a spiritual utility. Not logical consistency so much as relevance to felt human need is the test of its validity. Changes in creeds are dictated

[1] *Types of Modern Theology,* Charles Scribner's Sons, pp. 244-245.

by changes in the human situation as discerned by sensitive minds. Professor Mackintosh might have added that Kierkegaard's formulation of the doctrine of faith grew in part, at least, out of the tragedy of his own life. This suggests that theology is always in danger of becoming overweighted by fortuitous elements in the individual experience of the theologians themselves. But it is equally true that no theological systems would have been formulated but for critical experiences in the lives of individuals who were led by such experiences to reorganize their thinking and to redirect it in accord with insights which authenticated themselves in the experience of their fellows.

Again, it is no accident that the new orthodoxy has assailed the concern of liberal Christianity with "experience," and opposed the whole stream of thought that flows from the teaching of Schleiermacher. In a time of great social stress and disillusionment men turn almost instinctively away from the present, the tentative, the experimental, the adventurous, and seek security in what is "forever" established and therefore needs no validation in contemporary human experience. There is, I think, an obvious fallacy here in that their own experience is, after all, the most significant factor in their theological position. It is the experience of frustration that engenders a demand for something wholly unconditioned by human effort. A need for security drives men to seek it in something remote from the scene of their confusion and discomfiture. I believe the entire frame-work of apocalypticism in religious history rests on the experience of defeat in the ordering of human affairs. Had there been no destruction of Jerusalem, no Exile in Jewish history, there would probably have been no apocalyptic Hebrew literature such as we find in Daniel, in Revelation, in the Apocrypha and in portions of the Gospels. The development of Jewish apocalyptic reflects throughout the vicissitudes of Jewish history. Had there been no disastrous war in Europe a quarter-century ago we should not be confronted with a theology which puts so nearly exclusive emphasis on the otherness of God. Because theology is so definitely a rendering of personal experience and because such experience is so varied, there is always at hand the doctrinal material with which a new religious concern may give itself intellectual clothing in the form of a creed. It is small wonder that in the hour of postwar tragedy a spirit like Karl Barth should have turned to Kierkegaard's dialectical theology for conceptual support of the human need he accurately sensed for a God far above the battle. This is another way of saying that the Barthian theology can be interpreted only by invoking the principle of historical relevance which that theology has so often denied. The doctrine was born in the pressure of a situation, the urgency of an ethical concern for the enthronement of God in the affairs of men. All religious movements acquire their vigor at the expense of valid emphases in other movements which their immediate concern has obscured. Their very strength is due to the existence of particular factors in the historical situation in which they emerge. Their "truth" is in their spiritual drive, not in the ultimate validity of their creeds.

Where Christianity has suffered from dogmatism, that result has been due mainly to the false abstraction of ideas from their "operational" context. Theologians are indispensable but when they become a self-regulating "gild" of abstract thinkers they become obscurantist. Theology as "queen of the sciences" has sometimes fostered a kind of "lese majesty"! This is nothing less than abrogation of the principle of utility in spiritual affairs.

Indeed, much light can be thrown on theological inquiry from the history of science. Science has its purely theoretical concepts, but they are valued in accord with the degree of success they make possible in the further exploration of reality. Ultimately, the rise and fall of doctrines can be explained in no other way than by reference to the principle of utility. It is unfortunate that our dislike of the philosophic word pragmatism should have obscured the "pragmatic" element in all doctrinal Christianity—the submission of all creeds to the test of experience. For this is precisely what the Church has always done. Dr. McGiffert once said that the great theological controversies of history have not been settled, but relegated. When a doctrinal point ceases to be debated—the validity, for example, of filioque in the Creed, upon which Christendom divided, or the vital difference between homoousias and homoiousias on which the issue at Nicea turned—it is not because one concept has been finally accepted but because the issue no longer mightily matters.

There is no reason why the submission of doctrines to repeated tests in terms of experience should be confused with skepticism or tentativeness concerning the spiritual values which they mediate. To conceive the history of Christian thought as a mere genealogy of ideas is a falsification of history itself. Professor Becker in a study of eighteenth-century thought has noted what he charmingly calls "a favorite pastime of those who interest themselves in the history of culture to note the transfer of ideas (as if it were no more than a matter of borrowed coins) from one writer to another."[2] It is probably truer to say that ideas are neither created nor destroyed by other ideas: they are called forth by necessity and are relegated and superseded as they cease to be relevant to what people are concerned about.

[2] Carl L. Becker, *The Heavenly City of the Eighteenth Century Philosophers*, Yale University Press, p. 72.

Yet there is a lag in this process of historical validation or rejection, owing to a certain inertia of concepts that have once gained currency. Life moves faster than thought, for purpose is prior to thinking. Hence, we are continually confronted with complaints from laymen that Christian doctrines seem to lack reality. The consequence of this lay indifference is not complimentary to the clergy. For the common response of the minister to it has been one of accommodation—a discontinuance of doctrinal preaching and teaching with a rather uneasy conscience for so doing. Instead of undertaking the difficult task of theological reconstruction which would mean finding new forms by which to express the real concerns of the Christian community, we have followed the easier course of finding the nearest equivalents for Christian conceptions in the cultural milieu of humanitarianism and letting these stand in place of definitely Christian affirmations concerning God, man and the world. Let me repeat, unless there are such affirmations that have validity for the Christian community as such, authenticating themselves in the life of that community, then the survival of Christianity is no more than an example of cultural inertia.

The authority of religious doctrines is precisely the power and significance of the cumulative experience which they symbolize. Dr. Charles Clayton Morrison has given an impressive statement of this relationship: "This historical community is coming to be the field of modern theology. The new thinking has abandoned the search for God in psychological experience and in the cosmos, because it now sees that both psychology and cosmology deal only with abstractions—that experience is only our human response to something which comes to us from beyond experience, something objective, something *given,* something which comes to us *to be experienced by our participation in it.* Theology is now asking what that Something *is.* It does not find its answer in a transcendental cosmos, but in history, in that continuing historical community which has come down to us as the Christian church, in which it sees God actually working to reconcile the world unto himself."[3] There can be no Christian theology apart from the insights of a historic community which is ever on the march.

This close identification of conceptual thinking with the experience of a community is basic to an understanding of the social gospel. For essentially that gospel means that Christianity is concerned not merely with individuals, not merely with individuals in relation to others, but with the structure of the community itself. It means that the common life has a primary, not a de-

[3] "The 'Field' of Modern Theology" in *Christendom,* Winter, 1939, Vol. IV, No. 1, p. 42.

rived, importance. More will be said on this point when we come to discuss the Church. For the present it will suffice to say that the Christian social gospel gets whatever validity it has not from any emphasis on altruism or even on respect for individual personality—ethical religions always stress these—but rather from the fact that it proposes to Christianize the world not in atomistic fashion, by changing individuals one at a time, but by refashioning the structure of human relationships, by the building of a spiritual community in which personality can grow. In other words, the social gospel proposes to synchronize individual and social redemption. Its conspicuous weakness has been its failure to recognize the tragic conflict that goes on in the will of man, and the personal ground of social redemption.

Insistence on the historical relevance of doctrines and the resulting limits of their validity is in no sense a disparagement of theology. An adequate Christian ethic must have an adequate theological base. A nihilistic attitude toward theology is of a piece with disregard for all conceptual thinking. It is through symbols that meanings are mediated. Language itself is an elaborate symbolism, essential not only to communication but to thinking as well. And doctrines are vehicles for rendering timeless truth in concrete, that is, in historical, terms. It is when a man gains an insight into something significant for him *as man*, in terms of its relevance to

[26]

a historical situation of which he is himself a part, that he fastens himself to a doctrine. A doctrine is a statement that has passed over from the indicative to the imperative mood in the heat of man's striving to come to terms with the world as it confronts him in the present. This is why it has been said that multitudes of men will die for a dogma, but none will die for a conclusion. Fervent belief is the dynamic for action. As Professor Moffatt has said concerning the early Church, "Nothing is more clear in the fourth century than the historical principle that, while causation is much less simple in the moral, historical order than in the physical, it was the central beliefs of the corporate Church that for the most part determined its social implications and attitudes."[4]

Such reflections as these disclose the great difficulty of the task of theological thinking. On the one hand is the unquenchable religious and ethical urge for ultimates; on the other is the fact, documented abundantly in the history of civilization, that creeds stoutly held today as ultimate and unquestionable become debatable tomorrow and may be discarded the day after tomorrow. It will perhaps be startling to some to be told that the formula drafted by the World Council of Churches as a test for inclusion—acceptance of Jesus Christ "as

[4] James Moffatt, *The First Five Centuries of the Church*, Cokesbury Press, pp. 167-168.

God and Savior"—was regarded as a heresy in the early Church, doing violence to a trinitarian faith. The mature person is one who can make doctrine his instrument and not his master. He must know full well that the form of statement he gives to his religious experience will not satisfy persons whose need is different because their situation is different. How then can he attribute that ultimate validity to his creed which will give it heat enough to motivate his life? How can one age assign validity to a conceptual structure which must have a quality of certainty to make it effectual but which in the nature of the case is *dated* by the fact of its historical relevance? This is a perennial problem in religious thinking.

My contention is, of course, that such certainty never inheres in words and phrases but in the inner witness of a moral response. Let us illustrate the matter by reference to the doctrine of the Eucharist in Christianity. Ecumenical conferences always include representatives of communions whose beliefs concerning the Eucharist differ so sharply that they cannot possibly all be right in any factual sense. Not only so, but sitting with the sacramentarians are Quakers who hold none of these beliefs and insist that they are nonessential. The only way to rationalize such a situation is by reference to the central idea in the Eucharist, which is the "Presence." But that is an experience, and as such is self-validating.

The Quakers arrive at it in their own way, as something unmediated. The validity of the various doctrines of the Eucharist, on the other hand, is attested by the actual mediation of that experience which they effect. They are as "true" as they are effective; for the Quakers they are not true at all because they are not relevant to the Quaker type of experience—which, be it noted, is sufficiently like that of the sacramentarians so that they can worship together!

I am aware that many persons will at once pronounce this reasoning "pragmatic," and as such reject it. But, as I have been trying to say, Christianity has always been—in fact, though not consciously or avowedly—as pragmatic in respect to its creeds as it has been transcendentalist in its conception of reality. This distinction is of the utmost importance, and it should be obvious. We have courses in our theological schools in the history of doctrine, recognizing that dogmas follow each other across the pages of history. Yet we contend sharply over the letter of a current creed while we smile at those we have outgrown. Recognition that the meaning of a creed is in the experience it mediates would make possible the reverent use of such symbolism in a religious community for which it is vital without pressure upon others to adopt it.

All of which is extremely pertinent to the rethinking of the Christian social ethic in our time. For we have come upon a period of skepticism with reference to assumptions current among us for a generation, and many voices are raised in the interest of an uncritical return to older formulations as a substitute for the more difficult task of theological reconstruction. This demand is the despair of many Christian liberals seeking fellowship in the ecumenical movement. We cannot deal evasively with the historical process.

In an impressive book, *A Personalist Manifesto,* to which we shall have occasion to refer again, Emmanuel Mounier states our problem in terms of the conditions requisite for valid action. "An action has value and efficacy," he says, "only if it takes into account the significant truth of things and if it likewise considers the living historical situation which assigns to this action its proper place as well as its conditions of realization. The moment we are pressed to action on all sides under pretext of urgency no matter how or in what regard we act, it becomes a prime necessity to recall these two fundamental demands of action, truth and historical situation, and to satisfy them."[5] Here we are confronted with the fact of polarity in human thinking about values. There is "truth," and there is the "historical situation." The situation itself, by its very contemporaneousness, cannot fully comprehend truth. It is this fact that makes a pragmatist philosophy as often

[5] Longmans, Green & Co., page 3.

stated unsatisfactory; it lacks the dimension of time. On the other hand, the situation has in it essential novelty—a new incidence, so to speak, of something timeless. History has been called a process of concretion, of rendering in particular something that transcends the moment of time. There must always be something to "concrete." It is of the essence of religious faith that life has meaning; that it has a cosmic reference; that moral distinctions matter infinitely; that the struggle for the vindication of principles which, as William James said, "feels like a real fight," *is* a real fight; that man can relate himself to "something ongoing in the universe." Such considerations give content to truth in its aspect of timelessness. This truth is not like scientific "truths" because it lies outside the categories of verifiable fact: it can only be validated in experience as we address ourselves to a historical situation.

If the view taken here is tenable, all theological thinking thus reflects *situation* and at the same time discloses continuity in that the values which dogmas are designed to mediate are values which press for recognition in every age. They are not fortuitous: they inhere in the nature of man and the world, in human life as such. This remains true no matter what metaphysical view one holds as to the structure of the universe, whether it is "one or many." It remains true whether one stresses a transcendentalist or an immanentist view of God. But religious faith must be rendered through concepts which make it relevant to time and place, or man becomes lost in the historical process. Divergent views about the structure of reality—metaphysical doctrines—are situation-determined. They reflect varying philosophical outlooks. At the same time they have continuity in that they seek to make relevant to a particular time needs of the human spirit that continue from one age to another. Professor Hocking once told his students of philosophy that as they studied the various philosophical systems they would find themselves to some extent at home in all of them! The same may be said of the many systems of religious doctrine. The key to understanding them is to be found in the values they were designed to mediate at the time they caught the imagination of men. That *is* their effective meaning. And because human life has continuity in terms of meaning, doctrinal formulations are but the expression of concerns that are always in some degree present but are always shifting in priority and emphasis as history unfolds. By pulling out different stops, so to speak, in the great organ of human life, we can recover all the overtones that it has ever given forth. Yet today's mood and yearning call for today's music.

The reason for this discussion, as suggested above, is that the effort to state a Christian social ethic today is hampered by the impact of a theology that is relevant to one historical situation upon a way of thinking that is relevant to another. Thus far the ecumenical movement has been slowed down because of the effort to iron out conceptual differences by a process of mutual intellectual accommodation. This cannot be fruitfully undertaken without a prior appraisal of religious need in the experience of men. When churches that are indigenous to different countries undertake such a joint theological exploration, not only temporal but spatial factors have to be considered. For history is a manifold, or, to put it differently, there is not one history but many histories. Cultural development has differential rates of growth and there are many divergences when one country is compared with another—particularly when one continent is compared with another. When we consider the state of the Confessional Church in Germany during recent years—Niemöller in lonely isolation, and his comrades suffering spiritual incarceration—we may well ask how they could prophesy in any other terms than those of extreme transcendentalism, proclaiming the word of a God who seems far removed from the world which presses in upon them. I think I should be ready to defend the proposition that, given the situation in which he found himself, everything that Karl Barth has said is true! It is for this reason that I feel so strongly the inadequacy of current theological controversy. Much of it is irrelevant precisely because it seeks to find formulas that are, as one writer has put it, "true no matter what." There is no system of theology, no system of philosophy, that is "true no matter what." If there were, we might use the same textbooks decade after decade, and listen to the same sermons—which laymen sometimes complain that they do. The values that doctrines mediate are indeed timeless, as attested by religious experience, but the formulas have to be revamped again and again.

It is interesting to note that the necessary relevance of theology to history is illustrated by a recent statement of Barth himself. Commenting on Niemöller's offer to fight on the Nazi side, he said, "Do not forget that Niemöller has always been, and remains today, a good—a too good—German. In the war of 1914-18 he fought bravely, convinced of the right of the German cause. Later he became a pastor, and a very devout and faithful one. But his old Adam—as in all of us—is not dead. At the same time as being a fervent and irreproachable herald of the gospel message, he has never ceased to be a fervent German nationalist. . . . Do not forget that Niemöller is also a good—a too good—Lutheran. Lutheranism permits and demands the belief that there is a real chasm between the ecclesiastical and the political. At the bottom of this strange act of Niemöller's you will find the Lutheran dualism between the Kingdom of Heaven and the kingdom of the secular powers; between the gospel and the law; between God revealed in Jesus Christ and God working in nature and through history. . . . There are some German theologians and Christians who are free of the ingredients of this doctrine. There are just a few, you may be sure. But I fear that Niemöller was never one of this small number. He is capable of letting himself be put to death by Hitler in the cause of Christ, but he is also capable of being an officer on a warship of that same Hitler."[6]

Here is striking evidence of the way in which a theology of transcendence and nonrelevance to history explodes into relevance when confronted with a major ethical imperative. Many readers of Barth's most recent utterances have felt that he was at long last repudiating Barthianism! In a sense this is probably true. Consider, for example, his interpretation, in a book published a few years ago, of Paul's admonitions to the Corinthians. "In Corinth," he says, "the testimony of Christ is threatening to become an object of energetic human activity, a vehicle of real human needs." The deliverance on Niemöller, quoted above, is a far cry from this. As the pressure of political events grows stronger he is forced to recognize a principle of "relevance" in the gospel which he earlier denied—or at least seemed to

[6] Quoted in *The Christian Century*, March 6, 1940, Vol. LVII, No. 10, p. 301.

deny. Yet to him there appears no contradiction. The centrality of "decision" in Christian living he has always recognized. When a crucial ethical situation appears—when a choice must be made that matters to Almighty God—then the relevance of Christianity even to political affairs becomes so irresistible that Barth accepts it as something he has always believed! Such an utterance, however, illuminating as it is in terms of our present inquiry, is not to be taken as evidence that Continental theology is likely to remake itself quickly into an adequate expression of a Christian social ethic for our time.

In America we are feeling the impact of European thinking and it has gained in strength in proportion as the frustration which it symbolizes is experienced among us. But to say that such thought forms are normative is to say that the situation itself is normal. My contention is that in proportion as we desire to keep alive in America the mood, the purpose, the ethical movement to which democratic Christian liberalism has given support we should foster a structure of conceptual thought that is consistent with it. This involves not negation of theological systems as such, but selective treatment of what may be called the Christian theological heritage. For the great Christian imperatives are ethical, and in the final appraisal ethical adequacy is the test of theological validity. And ethical adequacy can be attained only as regard is had for the tasks with which the Christian community finds itself confronted. It follows that failure to give conceptual support to authentic ethical drives will outmode and outlaw any dogma. Dogmas have been thus relegated in the past and so they will be relegated again.

I am intrigued by the explicitness with which so eminent an exponent of the new orthodoxy as Professor Emil Brunner has recognized the necessity for continual theological adaptation. In a charmingly colloquial discussion of the present task of theology he says: "No theology is ever final, and the limitations of every age call for the corrections of the next. . . . God created man, and sinful man is the same Adam in all ages. The essence of natural man is identical throughout the times. But that does not mean that in every respect man is the same. As you know, this is not so. There is some difference between the men who first settled in this country and the ones who are populating the city of New York today. To put it in drastic fashion: not only we, but also the devil is progressive. He uses different weapons in different times; he also knows what rearmament is. . . .

"Therefore we have to ask in our age: where does the man of today stand and how, in consequence, has the gospel message to be presented to him? Not in order to make it agreeable to him, but in order to hit him with the word of divine judgment and to comfort him with the saving word of grace. This question of approach is of much more importance than a theology which still fosters the ideal of timelessness is prepared to admit. And so, as theologians we have to make a study of modern man. . . . A bad preacher he is who does not know his time."[7]

It may seem like a novel and gratuitous suggestion that theology has made trouble for itself by taking on a spurious similitude of physical science, but I believe this is true. Traditional orthodoxy makes little distinction between the assertion that God *is* and the assertion that the world *is*. That is to say, objective existence is affirmed in the one case in the same mode as in the other. God becomes object in the same sense as a physical object. A passage from the writings of Nicolas Berdyaev, one of the great philosophers of the Eastern Orthodox Church and an important figure in the ecumenical movement, is very illuminating at this point. He writes: ". . . Spirit is not another actuality, but it informs actuality with purpose. Spirit is, as it were, a Divine breath, penetrating human existence and endowing it with the highest dignity, with the highest quality of existence, with an inner independence and unity. An objective interpretation of spiritual reality

[7] "The Present-Day Task of Theology," in *Religion in Life*, Spring, 1939. Copyright 1938. By permission of The Abingdon Press, pp. 182-183.

raises the question: Do my spiritual states and experiences correspond to any authentic reality or are they merely subjective states? But this is a fundamentally false presentation of the problem, one based on the supposition that the subject should reflect some sort of object. Actually, spiritual states do not correspond to anything, they simply *are*: they are the prime reality, they are more existential than anything reflected in the objective world."[8] It will be recalled that one of Barth's prime contentions is that God is always Subject, never Object. Tillich also finds difficulty in predicating objective existence of God. This contrast between the new orthodoxy, on the one hand, and the old orthodoxy and liberal Christianity, on the other, is due, I think, to an insight on the part of the former that is of vast significance. What religious faith affirms is not objective facts but realities that transcend the factual realm. Religion and science are qualitatively different though the spheres of each fall within one framework of human experience. When religion has confused itself with science it has always experienced discomfiture. When it has invaded the realm of objective "existences," as the scientist uses that term, it has always had to retreat—just as science has had to retreat when it has tried to assimilate to its categories the spiritual values by which men live.

[8] *Spirit and Reality,* Charles Scribner's Sons, pp. 6-7.

God does not meet us, says Professor Baillie, "as one among many objects of our knowledge." "He is not part of the world we know—there is nothing that is more deprecated by the Barthian theologians than the tendency to make God *ein Stück Welt* [a piece of the world]—rather is He another Knowledge of that world. He confronts us not as an It nor as an inference from all possible Its, but, from the very beginning, as a Thou."[9]

I think that Kierkegaard's doctrine of the "existential moment" is relevant here. The object of faith is never something affirmed as "out there." The existential reference is to life, the life of the believer, here and now, in the historical moment. *"To be related to spirit,"* he says in a characteristic passage, *"means to undergo a test;* to believe, to wish to believe, is to change one's life into a trial; daily test is the trial of faith. —Yet one can preach on that score till doomsday to cowardly, effeminate unspiritual natures, they do not understand it, they do not really want to understand it. It seems to them that it is good enough if someone else takes the risk, and then they follow him—giving their assurance. But take the risk themselves—no thank you."[10] But, as Dr. Douglas Macintosh points out, this way of putting it—"not by arguing but by trying" is the essence of empiricism. It

[9] John Baillie. *Our Knowledge of God,* Charles Scribner's Sons, p. 220.

[10] *The Journals of Søren Kierkegaard,* a selection edited and translated by Alexander Dru. Entry 1044, Oxford University Press, p. 368.

has much closer affinity with American experimentalist philosophy than with the current European orthodoxy. To my mind nothing could illustrate better the fallacy in the assumption that liberalism and orthodoxy completely exclude each other and must be considered in either—or fashion.

The new orthodoxy has a richer equipment of philosophical conceptions than the old. Again and again in these pages they will be referred to, because I believe a synthesis of thought is under way which will on the one hand remedy the defect of philosophical shallowness in liberal Christianity and will on the other hand remove from the new orthodoxy the blight of metaphysical dualism which keeps God out of the historical process.

The interdependence of opposing systems of thought and their possible contribution to each other is beautifully illustrated in Nicolas Berdyaev's dedication of his book *Christianity and the Class War*. "I dedicate this book," he writes, "to Karl Marx who was the social master of my youth and whose opponent in ideas I have now become." Berdyaev has become one of the most influential interpreters of Christian philosophy in Europe, but his early orientation toward the struggle for human freedom he has never lost.

Chapter II

THE NATURE OF THE
CHRISTIAN ETHIC

WE STARTED out on a quest for a more authentic theological basis for the Christian social ethic than liberal Christianity has furnished. By way of clearing the ground we have considered the uses and limitations of creeds. This seemed necessary in the light of the widespread tendency to assume that the quest of a theology is equivalent to a reaffirmation of ancient formulas. The position taken, and supported by excerpts from neo-orthodox writings which are commonly overlooked, was that theology is always both an affirmation of truths believed to be timeless and a continual restatement of those truths in new doctrinal forms; also that the test of the validity of all such creedal formulations is their ethical adequacy in terms of relevance to historical situations. I am less interested in contending that this should be so than in pointing out that it is so, and therefore that to oppose the continual reconstruction of theology is useless obscurantism.

It is a noteworthy fact that the Christian community holds steadfastly to certain affirmations which persist in spite of the changing character of its creeds. If any proof were needed that this is true the ecumenical conferences held during the past few years should furnish convincing evidence. Perhaps the most impressive feature of these conferences has been what participants called the experience of *Una Sancta*—the demonstration of a spiritual unity which overshadowed the most stubborn doctrinal differences. The inescapable fact was the realization that the representatives of widely divergent and seemingly irreconcilable doctrinal positions found themselves—in some cases, perhaps, almost against their wills—gravitating toward a common center of Christian faith. In spite of what they said as theologians they found themselves to be participants in a common body of essential beliefs. That this experience preceded and quite outran all efforts at intellectual formulation of a consensus is precisely what, on the assumption I am making, was to be expected. "We are different; we disagree mightily; but we are one!" This is what they seemed to be saying. Even extreme liberals, who found the Continental theology not so much objectionable as unintelligible, were caught in the experience of spiritual unity. How shall this be accounted for?

My answer is that Christianity has one central truth, one abiding contribution to make to the religious life of the world, and only one. That contribution is Jesus Christ himself. The gospel *is* Jesus Christ. He is prior to all theologizing, and vaster than all creeds. The validity of Christianity is precisely the validity of what is revealed in his life and in his teaching. All through Christian history the authority of creeds has given way before the testimony of men and women who have been awakened by contact with that revealing personality and have declared, "One thing I know, that whereas I was blind, now I see."

I believe that right here we have the answer to the most fundamental theological question of our day: What validity can be claimed for revelation if a modern evolutionary view of the world be accepted? The cleavage between liberal and orthodox Christianity lies just here. The orthodox theologian takes refuge in the affirmation that the truths he holds are revealed. The liberal has demanded to know the criteria of revelation. How does it happen that something is revealed to one person, or one sect, and not to another? To whom and under what circumstances does "the Word" come? The inability on the part of orthodox theologians to give convincing answers to these questions repels liberal minds, and the result is that the very word "revelation" is suspect among large numbers of sincere Protestants.

I am disposed to think that this persistent controversy

is due to a strange rigidity in modern thinking, which is the fruit of a century or more of naïve mechanistic science. While it would be a crude expedient to turn from religion to science for an understanding of the spiritual, one must admit that some of the most liberating insights of our generation are coming from the scientists. It would be precarious as well as gratuitous to seek verification of religious affirmations in a scientific laboratory. Indeed, it is the testimony of scientists that this can *not* be done that seems to me so timely. A scientist's testimony to religious realities is precisely as weighty as that of any other person, no more so. But a scientist's testimony concerning the limits of his science should be helpful in dissipating crude ideas—both liberal and orthodox—of what "revelation" is. Mr. Einstein, in an address given a year or so ago to which little publicity was given, had this to say:

Those convictions which are necessary and determinant for our conduct and judgments, cannot be found solely along this solid scientific way.

For the scientific method can teach us nothing else beyond how facts are related to, and conditioned by, each other. The aspiration toward such objective knowledge belongs to the highest of which man is capable, and you will certainly not suspect me of wishing to belittle the achievements and the heroic efforts of man in this sphere. Yet it is equally clear that knowledge of what *is* does not open the door directly to what *should be*. One can have the clearest and most complete knowledge of what *is,* and yet not be able to deduce from that what should be the *goal* of our human aspirations. Objective knowledge provides us with powerful instruments for the achievement of certain ends, but the ultimate goal itself and the longing to reach it must come from another source. And it is hardly necessary to argue for the view that our existence and our activity acquire meaning only by the setting up of such a goal and of corresponding values. The knowledge of truth as such is wonderful, but it is so little capable of acting as a guide that it cannot prove even the justification and the value of the aspiration towards that very knowledge of truth. Here we face, therefore, the limits of the purely rational conception of our existence.

But it must not be assumed that intelligent thinking can play no part in the formation of the goal and of ethical judgments. When someone realizes that for the achievement of an end certain means would be useful, the means itself becomes thereby an end. Intelligence makes clear to us the interrelation of means and ends. But mere thinking cannot give us a sense of the ultimate and fundamental ends. To make clear these fundamental ends and valuations, and to set them fast in the emotional life of the individual, seems to me precisely the most important function which religion has to perform in the social life of man. And if one asks whence derives the authority of such fundamental ends, since they cannot be stated and justified merely by reason, one can only answer: they exist in a healthy society as powerful traditions, which act upon the conduct and aspirations and judgments of the individuals; they are there, that is, as something living, without its being necessary to find justification for their existence. They come into being not through demonstration but through revelation, through the medium of powerful personalities. One must not attempt to justify them, but rather to sense their nature simply and clearly.[1]

Now it is this characterization of revelation upon which I would focus attention. Mr. Einstein is a naturalist in philosophy, but he recognizes a quality of human experience, an order of phenomena which are, so to speak, out of series with everything that wears the aspect of mechanism. Much consternation among liberals has been caused by the intrusion into theological discussion of such phrases as "eternity breaking into time," and "the unique Kairos." My contention is that those terms have validity in just this sense, that while there is an aspect of causal sequence in phenomena, which the word "temporal" denotes, there is also an aspect of discontinuity, of novelty, of "irruption," if you will, the supreme manifestation of which is personality. And personality literally "breaks into" the temporal order of events with creative power. Now Christianity exists as a force in the world because of the emergence of a supreme personality, whose impact on the life of

[1] *Information Service,* June 3, 1939, Vol. XVIII, No. 22. Federal Council of the Churches of Christ in America.

the world is his own authentication. The enduring truth of Christianity is in the intrinsic authority of the personality of Jesus Christ. The combined testimony of men to the validity of that personal "revelation" is more significant than anything that theologians have ever said about him. The Christian Church has had through the centuries and will continue to have just as much authority as the personality of its Founder has upon those who expose themselves to the influence of his life. The Christian message *is* Jesus Christ.

In no other way, it seems to me, can we explain the fact that the Christian community actually includes groups which have so little common ground in creedal terms. They are bound together by reverence for and allegiance to a Person. There is a growing feeling among Christians of divergent theological views that there is a moral urgency in what is called the ecumenical movement—a duty to realize unity, despite conflicting creeds. This, I believe, is the compulsion of a Christian revelation embodied in Jesus himself, which is self-validating among those who have committed themselves to what the early Christians called "the way." To the ecumenical mind a divisive theology is coming to have the character of sin.

The significance of all this for our discussion must be apparent. As soon as it is recognized that the Christian message is embodied in Jesus himself its social and

[48]

ethical character is inescapable. For Jesus' life is for Christians the demonstration *par excellence* of what goodness in human relations means. There is a social gospel only because the personality of Jesus makes such a terrific impact on the whole order of human relationships, and because its demands can never be met without a thorough reorganization of human affairs. His ethical challenge to the individual is so forceful as to satisfy the most rugged realism of the current orthodoxy: he "knew what was in man." But his challenge to society has inspired in every succeeding age revolutionary efforts to remake the world. His ministry "convinces the world of sin, of righteousness and of judgment." The Christian essentials are all there: man's kinship with God, the tragedy of sin, salvation through the power of redemptive love. The power of this revelation of personality supreme and triumphant is not dependent on historical evidences of particular events. It would remain a possession of the Christian community even though not a vestige of documentary evidence were left. All the reported miracles pale into insignificance before the miracle of the life that informs the entire literature that it inspired.

What this means, of course, is that the central truth in Christianity is the embodiment of deity—the bringing of the divine within the apprehension of the human. In philosophical language, it is the meeting of the essential and the existential in personality. The theological word for it is incarnation, and it has had different creedal expressions. One of them, the Virgin Birth, seems to have been originally a heretical doctrine which was later adopted because of its polemic value. But the timeless truth expressed is the bridging of the gulf between the divine and the human in what I have called the miracle of personality. The word "miracle" here is no mere figure of speech, it signifies the negation of mechanism as a key to reality. Personality is the locus of creativity and the figure of Jesus Christ which the Christian community offers to the world represents the complete transfiguration of the human into the divine. In Jesus Christ, as the Church knows him, Hellenic and Palestinian traditions are fused, so to speak, and the timeless is embodied in the historical. Jesus of Nazareth *was,* Christ *is.* It is a grievous error on the part of liberals to dispense with New Testament Christology, for it is in the Pauline contribution to Christianity that we have the investiture of a historical character with the permanent quality of indwelling godhood. This insight, the Christian community believes, is a permanent addition to man's store of religious knowledge. The essential truth thus disclosed is that man is under an absolute mandate to express divinity in his own nature and in his whole life. The authority of Christianity at any time is precisely what the commanding figure of Christ achieves when presented to the world. Thus the Christian ethic is at once the simplest and the profoundest thing in the world—the impact of a perfected personal will on the consciences of men.

All defects in this or that theological system which Christians from time to time have formulated flow from failures to do justice to the lordship of Jesus. As insights into the meaning of that life and its implications for the lives of men have grown deeper one doctrine after another has been relegated or materially revised. The test of current creeds is the adequacy of their mediation to men's minds of the spirit of the Master Person. If the social gospel has been faulty in its theology it is because some essential element in the portrayal of the supreme Personality is lacking. I think one such element is not difficult to locate. Preoccupation with the revolutionary social implications of the life of Jesus has overshadowed the need for individual discipleship which takes on "the stature of the fullness of Christ." Nothing is clearer in the teaching of Jesus than that virtue is inward, that righteousness is only rags if it does not clothe a loving heart. There is no social virtue that does not become internalized in a devoted and disciplined life.

It cannot be too often said that the Christian ethic is not a matter of balancing two emphases, the individual and the social. We get nowhere by insisting that *both* the individual *and* the social must receive attention. This is likely to lead to tightrope walking. If the Gospel is not apprehended in its bipolar character it is not apprehended at all. Recall for a moment that well-to-do young man who came to Jesus to learn what else he might have to do beside living a very exemplary life (and being in good religious standing, too, for he had "kept the commandments"). He was told to devote his possessions to relieving the needs of his fellow men. When he couldn't take it did Jesus tell him he was *half* right? There is no record of it. The interview ended and he went away—all wrong. That is one side of the picture. Now recall that stern reminder from the pen of Saint Paul: "Though I bestow all my goods to feed the poor . . . and have not love, it profiteth me nothing."

We come now to a consideration of the Christian social hope, and to the much debated question what actual social reference Jesus' ethical teachings had. If the central thing in the Gospel is the life of Christ, in deed and in word, then we can find no valid Christian ethic which cannot be derived by an inevitable logic from the total impact of his life upon the world. This being the case, the immediate reference of Jesus' sayings—in what sense they were apocalyptic or eschatological and in what sense of permanent social significance—is not determinative for his followers. Mankind in general has recognized an intrinsic authority in them without reference to these doctrinal issues. Nevertheless, in a time when the practical implications of his teachings for social ethics are a matter of sharp dispute the problem must be considered. The argument of Schweitzer on this point is familiar to most biblical students. He held in his well-known work *The Quest of the Historical Jesus* that Jesus' teachings must be interpreted entirely in the light of his apparent acceptance of the apocalyptic outlook which characterized his age. To Schweitzer all the ethical absolutes in Jesus' teachings ("If one would . . . take away your coat, let him have your cloak also"; "Give to him that asketh of you"; etc.) must be viewed as reflecting the current preoccupation with the consummation of history: the time is short. Thus Jesus' ethic becomes an "interim ethic." This view has been sharply challenged by other writers and, as Schweitzer stated it, has been largely discredited. He sought to prove too much. Professor Wilder, who has recently surveyed the literature of the subject, finds Jesus quite unbound by any such rigid apocalyptic framework and insists that there are abundant evidences that often in his teachings he assumed the indefinite continuance of the world order. Yet Professor Wilder concludes that Jesus presented "the inbreaking future"—to which the element of crisis in his teaching is due—"usually in apocalyptic terms." He avoids the "interim ethic" assumption as an explanation of Jesus' radical precepts by regarding them not as ethical generalizations, but as "occasional utterances to particular persons which the sacred records have lifted out of the obscurity of their original moment."[2]

Professor Douglas Clyde Macintosh has also been wrestling with this problem and likewise repudiates the interpretation that Schweitzer popularized. His explanation of the "absolutes" is accomplished by a simple appeal to common sense. It must be admitted, he says, "that Jesus himself recognizes even if he does not very explicitly teach an interim ethic. But it is not the interim ethics of Schweitzer's interpretation. . . . In fact it is the exact opposite. While Schweitzer says the Sermon on the Mount is a compilation of ethical teachings never intended to have more than temporary validity, and not really having even that, since what they presupposed was all a mistake, the truth is that the Sermon on the Mount gives expression to the absolute, universal and eternal ideal for the conduct of persons in society, but that this ideal becomes more and more fully realizable by us the more it is being realized in other individuals and *in the organization of society*."[3] This,

[2] Amos Niven Wilder, *Eschatology and Ethics in the Teaching of Jesus,* Harper & Brothers, p. 244.

[3] Douglas Clyde Macintosh, *Social Religion,* Charles Scribner's Sons, p. 61.

of course, may be objected to by strict constructionists as gratuitous. It is admittedly an importation of a "common-sense" rule in biblical interpretation.

To me it seems that this appeal to common sense is all to the good, but if admitted at all, it may carry us out of bounds so far as the scholars' controversy is concerned. Is there not a certain artificiality in this exegetical inquiry? It is much too facile to dissolve away the absolute quality of Jesus' ethical precepts by referring them all to an apocalyptic expectation, but are we not compelled to recognize that a world view so foreshortened as was that of Jesus' time could not fail to influence his teaching in a profound way? That the interim-ethic theory as presented is invalidated by the testimony of Christian history may be granted, but this does not entirely dispose of the matter. If Jesus' absolute precepts are not to be regarded as taking their perfectionist forms from the imminence of the end of history, are they still to be regarded as eschatological, referring to a heavenly kingdom rather than to the life that now is? The issue is important because of the current tendency to rob the concept of the Kingdom of God of all its developmental aspects and to give it meaning only in eschatological terms. (The issue is not whether there is the germ of an evolution theory in the Parable of the Leaven. Jesus was not a professor of philosophy. A reader not too sophisticated can see the flashes of a timeless ethic in Jesus' teaching and see equally well how hopelessly unrealizable that teaching is except as it becomes embodied in the social structure itself.)

Interestingly enough, the new orthodoxy rejects Schweitzer's apocalyptic interpretation in order to preserve the timeless character of Jesus' teachings but holds to an eschatological interpretation in order to maintain that the actualization of his precepts cannot occur within history, but only beyond history. The inevitable result, I think, is to lessen the ethical imperative. It may be admitted that the consummation of the Kingdom was, in the mind of Jesus, envisaged as beyond history, but that this fact is unrelated to his expectation that the end was rapidly approaching is hard to imagine. Had it not been for his sharing the contemporary apocalyptic expectation, I cannot avoid the belief that his teachings would not only have taken on a different form but would have had a much more explicit social and political reference. That he could ever have envisaged the consummation of the Kingdom of God within the historical process is not to be supposed. In spite of assertions to the contrary, no exponent of the social gospel, as far as I am aware, entertains any such idea. The notion of consummation in time is foreign to a developmentalist philosophy. But had Jesus not lived in the shadow of the apocalyptic doom, would not his entire ethical teaching have taken on more of the form of the Parable of the Leaven in the Meal rather than fluctuating between that and the contrasting form of the Parable of the Ten Virgins?

In any case I think Schweitzer's more recent comment on this subject is sound: "We must take the ethical religion of Jesus out of the setting of his worldview and put it in our own. Whereas he expected the kingdom of God to come at the end of the world, we must endeavor, under the influence of the spirit of his ethical religion, to make the kingdom of God a reality in this world by works of love."[4]

More important than any question of biblical criticism is the broader one of the significance of absolutes in the realm of ethics. Here the argument has to be addressed to that position so commonly held among liberals under the influence of the experimentalist philosophy according to which "all values are relative." I think this rests on a confusion of thought. The confusion occurs in the effort to frame a philosophy that will take account of the necessarily relative character of *attained* values and of practical value judgments. The ethical "absolutist" commonly assumes not merely the existence, conceptually speaking, of absolute good, not merely the reality of the absolute mandate, "Be ye per-

[4] Albert Schweitzer, "Religion in Modern Civilization," *Christian Century*, November 21, 1934, Vol. LI, No. 47, p. 1484.

fect," but also the possibility of embodying the absolute in particular choices. Thus he affirms that certain specific acts—participating in war, or taking profit in business, for example—are always necessarily wrong. The "relativist," on the other hand, maintains that the right course of action can be determined in a particular situation "on the merits," that is, on the basis of a judgment of consequences. Now I would contend that this practical relativism does not necessarily nor properly involve a nihilistic attitude toward ethical absolutes as "reals." This position is well supported in the thinking of religious empiricists and naturalists.

Consider, for example, the following from the able editor of the *Personalist*: "Just as in mathematics, the mathematical infinite presents a working principle exceedingly useful in achieving results, so there is an inner demand that morally and spiritually one must aim at perfection. The perfection aimed at can have no flaw, it must appear superhuman. These superhuman perfections are demanded as the attributes of God, the supreme reality. That superhuman perfections put a strain not only on human achievement but likewise on human understanding makes no whit less necessary the demand. . . .

"The religious man's dream of absolutely perfect moral conduct, unachieved, is no more reprehensible than the scientific search for absolute reality or the philosophical one of absolute truth. The only moral requirement is that he should honestly strive after it. The illusory character of these absolutes in practice is no evidence that they are not necessary and required. They will be until partial knowledge becomes complete, faith becomes sight and all hypotheses are either demonstrated or disproved. . . . Such capacity can be had only in a creature not quite absorbed in the temporal and material; one who is something more than the world in which he lives; one who transcends both time and matter and is himself creative. In personality the contradictory notions of immanence and transcendence, of essence and reality, find common ground. Whenever they coincide in man or God, you have personality."[5]

Again consider this statement by the late Professor Woodbridge, one of the most eminent naturalistic philosophers of his time: "In somewhat technical language, what philosophy and science both need to recognize is that not only are actualities real, but possibilities are real also. And it belongs to the idea of a possibility that, however real it may be, it may never become actual in the sphere of concrete experience. Consequently, if the realm of the possible is ever to be made available for our use in life, it must be laid hold of by other conceptions and other categories than those

[5] Ralph Tyler Flewelling, "The Need and the Illusion of Absolutes," *The Personalist*, Spring, 1940, Vol. 21, No. 2, pp. 125, 126, 128.

by means of which we formulate the actual in terms of positive, scientific knowledge. And it should be recognized that the attempt so to make the realm of the possible available is just as important, just as valid, just as necessary as the attempt to lay hold of scientific truth. If, then, the reality of our personality as a given psychological fact is to be made available by analyzing it into mental elements in correlation, how is the reality of our personality as a moral possibility to be made available?

"How has it been made available? The answer is, in the moral ideal and religious aspirations and beliefs of the race. We read in their history how man's possibilities have been revealed to him, how he has been inspired and helped toward their attainment. In such a ministry morality and religion have found their proper function."[6]

These citations are offered for the purpose, avowed at the beginning of these lectures, of showing that on the fundamental issues of ethics the cleavage in contemporary philosophical thinking is not so deep as is commonly assumed.

A baffling problem in Christian ethics which liberals have not squarely faced is the austere and inexorable aspect that life often wears. Liberal social Christianity

[6] Reprinted from Frederick J. E. Woodridge, *Nature and Mind,* by permission of Columbia University Press, p. 303.

undertakes to express the governorship of the world in terms of fatherly care. But much happens in the universe that even a stern father would not do. The physical universe presents a decidedly unmoral aspect. The winds and floods have no conscience. Furthermore, the moral universe often wears a stern retributive aspect which seems anything but benevolent and forgiving. Here we encounter the old and unsolved problem of theodicy—a justification of the ways of God to man. This is not the place for another feeble attempt at solution of it. I would point out, however, that an ethical system has to take account of the inexorable in the universe as well as the affable. Carlyle's often quoted comment concerning the lady who complacently remarked that she "accepted the universe" never grows stale. " 'Gad," said the salty Scot, "she'd better!" Now liberal Christianity has too generally sought to evade the inexorable by identifying God with the benevolent side of the universe and dissociating him from that intractable and baffling aspect of the world which Professor Brightman calls the Given. This concept has the merit of avoiding an ultimate dualism and locating the crucial ethical struggle within the divine nature. In a sense it may be said that the problem is one of reconciling the will of God with the nature of God.

To object to this idea because it predicates finiteness of the divine will—pitting the will of God against the

Given in the nature of God—is rather naïve, it seems to me. For the will of man limits the will of God, in any case. This is why there is an ethical struggle in the world. The very persistence of evil is a challenge to God. To fall back on the assumption that in some way God wills the evil can scarcely bring any satisfaction to a mature mind. What seems to be going on in the universe is a struggle to make the will of God dominant over the "Given" which limits that will. Such a view, at least, gives ethics an adequate framework by supplying a cosmic reference.

But what I wish to emphasize is the aspect of stern righteousness in the will of God itself which can scarcely be adequately characterized as benevolence. There is an implacability in the moral order. "Be not deceived; God is not mocked; whatsoever a man soweth that shall he also reap." Here is an aspect of existence which has to be set over against the assurance, "Like as a father pitieth his children so the Lord pitieth them that fear him." The ancient Hebrews understood this fully, as the penitential psalms testify. Justice no less than love has its place in the Christian ethic. The social gospel is not sentimental.

Here again the weakness of contemporary liberal Christianity is located in an inadequate, because partial, interpretation of the ministry of Jesus himself. It is true that the Christian ethic may be summed up in a declara-

which abides despite historical changes—with the same convincingness and finality that characterizes declaratory statements of fact.

It is interesting to note in passing that this use of myth makes tacit recognition of the instrumental nature of concepts. The new orthodoxy, in contrast to the old, distinguishes between its myths and its facts. To make a statement in factual form of something that is not a fact can be justified if at all only on the ground that it is the only way language affords of conveying the meaning that needs to be conveyed. From my point of view, nothing could illustrate better the fact that *use* is the paramount consideration in evaluating doctrinal statement. If the neo-orthodox mythology were defended consistently on this basis, by reference to the inadequacies of language in its present state, it would raise no fundamental issue. But when the conceptual device becomes identified with timeless truth itself the modern mind rebels. The theological myth is then put on a par with the pre-scientific myth.

Now it is doubtful whether the religious myth is essentially different from certain concepts in common use among scientists. In this connection, Professor Goodenough has referred to the Freudian concepts of the Id, the Ego and the Super-ego. These are symbols standing for tendencies toward specific kinds of behavior. Yet the psychologists who employ them seem to find them indispensable. The "genes" which the geneticists describe as the mechanisms of heredity may or may not be physical entities but whether they are or not is a matter irrelevant to the validity of the term in scientific parlance. The only merit the concept of a "luminiferous ether" ever had was the degree to which it facilitated description of phenomena which depended upon it only in a conceptual sense. But here is the important point: the competent scientist never confuses the linguistic expedient with the truth he seeks to convey, and the symbols in scientific discourse are discarded if and when they can be advantageously superseded.

The subject is important for us here not because the myth itself is suspect as a useful instrument but because current Christian orthodoxy may be emphasizing myths which have less validity as conceptual forms than in former times. I believe that lay Christianity in America is strongly of this opinion. What has been strangely overlooked is the fact that liberal Christianity no less than orthodoxy has a mythology which justifies itself on precisely the same grounds as orthodox mythology, but which is much more relevant to the conditions of modern life and thought.

Here we come to grips with the common charge that liberal social Christianity is romantic in that it makes unwarranted optimistic affirmations about "progress"— that it is, so to speak, socially perfectionist. Now in this critical view progress is regarded as a myth of a very different sort, a spurious myth. It may be remarked in passing that, as Professor Lyman has pointed out, any declaration that God has a redemptive purpose for the world which will be realized in his own time has affinities with the idea of progress. That is to say, if the world is undergoing redemptive change it would seem an arbitrary use of terms to deny progress in the historical process. The point here, however, is that the idea of progress toward a vividly pictured goal—and it is the tendency in liberal Christianity to dwell upon this "goal" that the new orthodoxy so strongly criticizes— may well be regarded as a sort of inverted myth, a myth with a forward rather than a backward reference. The conventional myth seeks to explain destiny by reference to derivation. The ethical myth in liberal social Christianity affirms destiny as a lively faith. It achieves vividness by reference to a goal described in terms of a historical consummation, but this inverted myth of social Christianity is not to be regarded as affirming a consummation within the historical process.

Consider, for example, the concept of the brotherhood of man as it comes to us through the Hebrew-Christian tradition. To base that ideal on the statement that God made "of one blood" all the races of men is to employ the conventional mythical device which is cast in the historical narrative form. But it is doubtful if the average modern mind is greatly helped by such a myth. The liberal Christian affirms human brotherhood, not as historic fact, and not as conventional myth, but as an ideal that embodies an ethical imperative. Reinhold Niebuhr himself said something of similar import when he wrote: "The assumption upon which religion proceeds is not scientific. All men are not brothers. They are, in fact, continually arrayed in warring camps, and they are frequently enemies rather than brothers. But potentially they are brothers, and to assume that they are, will help to make them so."[7] The question if and when this ideal will be fully and finally realized is irrelevant. The assertion that Christian social liberalism expects that this quest of a spiritual ideal will be fully consummated in time may be true of naïve and uncritical minds. Indeed to the extent that it is true, a resurgent, "realistic" orthodoxy performs a needed service. But it is fundamental to the liberal position that the *maintenance of a noble quest finds its warrant not in an anticipated consummation but in the rewards of creative endeavor*. Consummation *as event* is by very definition the negation of history. The one thing that life cannot tolerate is a static condition. What ethical action does require in conceptual terms

[7] Reprinted from *The Contribution of Religion to Social Work*, by permission of Columbia University Press, pp. 63-64.

is an "end" so clearly visualized that it justifies un-
stinted effort. To confuse this meaning of "ends" with
finality in time is to destroy their dynamic significance
as religious motives. Now the concept of progress
toward a goal actually conduces to ethical motivation.
The difference between this position and one that
makes the ethical struggle with the world merely a
mitigation of crudities in the mesh of human relations
about which, after all, little can be done is the difference
between a lively hope and the perpetual fighting off
of despair.

It was manifestly this that J. H. Muirhead had in
mind in his very appreciative review of Reinhold Niebuhr's *Moral Man and Immoral Society*. He finds the
argument tending toward a final dualism between
ethics and politics, of which he says: "It may be a
proof of the survival in me of the bourgeois romanticism which is here attacked, but there is 'a voice which
keeps humming in my ears' that to accept any such
view would be the acknowledgement of a moral defeatism in the world of politics to which I am loath
to find myself driven. . . . It is because of the promi-
nence given to this note that his book, so stimulating in
other respects, seems to me to be useful rather as another illustration of the present disillusionment with
regard to old hopes than as the inspiration of new

ones—into which by a difference of emphasis it might, I believe, without much difficulty have been turned."[8]

Having quoted these words it is a pleasure to insert passages from Mr. Niebuhr's own pen which seem to supply the missing quality: "Men cannot live," he writes, "without faith in the meaning of existence and without the effort to fulfill a meaning which is suggested but not yet realized. In pursuing this task they will sink into skeptical nihilism if they lose faith in an unconditioned good as a criterion of all historical values. Their faith will be corrupted into a cruel fanaticism if they imagine that they have captured and domesticated the eternal and the unconditioned; and it will degenerate into a morally impotent mysticism if they despair of history and flee to a realm of the absolute where all distinctions of good and evil become meaningless. The way of moral sanity and spiritual health is always a narrow one and must be followed on the edge of one abyss after another."[9]

Here again it is apparent that the controversy is a matter of emphasis. Theological issues seldom admit of an "either—or" solution. Every candid liberal must gladly acknowledge the service rendered by the orthodox revival in theology in forcing a re-examination of

[8] J. H. Muirhead, *Hibbert Journal*, Vol. XXXII, Oct., 1933-July, 1934, pp. 157-158.

[9] "The Return to Primitive Religion," *Christendom*, Winter, 1938, Vol. III, No. 1, p. 8.

liberalism. We have already had too much of metaphysical polemics over it. My contention is that all dogma must meet one test, the test of ethical fruitage. "No theories," said Rauschenbusch, "about the future of the Kingdom of God are likely to be valuable or true which paralyze or postpone redemptive action on our part."[10] It is my strong belief that to conceive the Kingdom of God as a *project within the historical process* which is motivated by reference to a goal never reached but always envisaged, is the most effectual way to implement the Christian ethical imperative in our day. Participation in Kingdom building is a self-validating experience. Rauschenbusch himself said the consummation of the Kingdom can come only "by the power of God in his own time." But he also declared that the Kingdom "is miraculous all the way, and is the continuous revelation of the power, the righteousness and the love of God." Only such a dynamic conception of the social meaning of Christianity can fire the imagination of an age that accepts, for man, moral responsibility for the state of the world. In a situation where action is blocked and where hope deferred makes the heart sick, a transcendentalizing of all religious values may give needed solace. For solace, even escape, has a place in human experience. It is doubtful, however, if on the whole, such a theological framework will prove

[10] *A Theology for the Social Gospel,* Macmillan Company, p. 141.

conducive in America to anything other than an ethical
alibi for those who want it but who should not have it,
while depressing those who have been eager for something to reinforce the "divine imperative" in human
affairs. If I am not mistaken there are signs already
that the genius of American Christianity is not going
to embody itself conceptually in a conventional mythological framework of the sort we have been discussing.

This discussion does not assume the ultimate superiority of one theological framework over another. Indeed it aims at substituting ethical adequacy for logical
finality as a theological criterion. Only on this basis
can a "gospel" claim to have any theology at all. If,
while recognizing the theological shallowness that has
characterized the social gospel in America, I nevertheless lean toward the liberal alternative to current orthodox declarations of belief, it is because I view the
historical situation in which liberal Christianity has
evolved as more nearly normative than that which
gave rise to the new orthodoxy. Nevertheless, whenever
human affairs are characterized by crisis it is to be expected that theology will take on a predominantly
"crisis" character. To say that the developmental conception of the Kingdom is truer than an eschatological
conception means only that orderly process is more
normative than catastrophic. But the point of this entire discussion will be lost if the necessity is not seen

for what I may call a higher—a nonapocalyptic—eschatology which furnishes a goal that lies beyond the historical process. Quite as necessary—and here, I repeat, liberal social Christianity has been very weak—is the preservation of the "crisis" element in human experience itself. And by crisis I mean here, conscious critical encounter between man and God.

To achieve this result requires a discipline which only the compulsions of a prophetic religion can activate. The social gospel has often been weak in the cultivation of this kind of dynamic motivation. And the reason is to be found in its preoccupation with the social task, the urgency of which its new vision disclosed. To say that it has neglected the individual is not as accurate or illuminating as to say that it has not realized the social significance of the penitential attitude which worship fosters and which keeps man under the sense of a divine imperative.

This brings us to what is admittedly the crux of the theological issue—the problem of transcendence. Liberal social Christianity is criticized as naturalistic and hence as making no recognition of the supernatural. Now this is true if the supernatural is defined as denoting one part of a universe that is dualistically conceived. If there are two worlds, qualitatively different, operating under different laws so that man's effort to unify and organize his experience is necessarily baffled on account of this boundary, then the assumptions of liberal Christianity are out of line with reality. The difference between the two conceptions has been well stated by John Macmurray: "It is one thing to realize that the world in which we live is wider and deeper than we know, and that there may be whole reaches of it and aspects of it which are hidden from our normal consciousness. It is quite another thing to hold that there is another world which is not this world at all. It is one thing to say that religion is about the other world. It is a very different thing to say that it is about an aspect of this world to which we are usually blind."[11]

Again, note this striking statement from Karl Heim, an outstanding European theologian who has stood close to Barth. "When we distinguish," he writes, "between Creator and creature, between transcendent and immanent, between God and the world, we are not marking out a boundary-line between two worlds or two departments of life, which lie adjacent to each other, or one above the other. Nor is this a boundary of dimension such as may be drawn between two 'spaces.' We are concerned, on the contrary, with a field of battle, a war-zone, in which two standpoints oppose each other, two contrary attitudes of Spirit, two

[11] *The Structure of Religious Experience,* Yale University Press, p. 67.

alternatives in regard to every question asked, one of which must be true and the other false."[12]

It is so easy to be tricked by phrases. If by the super-natural is meant something different from nature only as the super-organic differs from the organic, the issue is enormously simplified. Consider this statement by William Adams Brown: "Under the term 'nature' we sum up those recurrent experiences which, being found everywhere, lend themselves to classification and pre-diction. By the supernatural we mean the individual, the unpredictable, the creative. Natural theology deals with the universal in religion, revealed theology with those exceptional insights and experiences through which our discovery of the universal has been made. Neither is complete without the other. Among the disastrous rationalizations of history none has been more disastrous than that which has separated revealed theology as the study of living religion from the rational processes by which alone it can be interpreted and justified."[13]

The philosophy implicit in this is the philosophy of indeterminism—sometimes called emergence—which in turn is implicit in liberal social Christianity. Indeed, it may well be contended that the battle over supernaturalism, in the traditional sense of the word,

[12] *God Transcendent,* Charles Scribner's Sons, p. 216.
[13] *The Case for Theology in the University,* Charles Scribner's Sons, pp. 65-66.

was in reality ended in American philosophy with the elaboration of the concept of novelty or emergence as against the traditional mechanistic view. Mechanism was the real foe of religion, not naturalism. There is no necessary connection between naturalism and materialism. What modern religious naturalism seeks to do is to bring the creative aspect of life into an empirical framework—to domesticate religion within the common life. The *deus ex machina* is displaced by an informing creative force. Supernature becomes the self-transcending aspect of nature and of man.

At the risk of being badly misunderstood I plead for a new orientation in Christian thought toward this central philosophic problem. It is far from my purpose to suggest that the distinctive elements in Christianity should be diluted with "nature religion." I have insisted, rather, that the central truth in Christianity is the revelation in the person of Christ himself. But by what right or reason shall a Christian theologian condemn, because he is a "naturalist," the man who wrote this?

> O world, thou choosest not the better part!
> It is not wisdom to be only wise,
> And on the inward vision close the eyes,
> But it is wisdom to believe the heart.
> Columbus found a world, and had no chart,
> Save one that faith deciphered in the skies;
> To trust the soul's invincible surmise
> Was all his science and his only art.

> Our knowledge is a torch of smoky pine
> That lights the pathway but one step ahead
> Across a void of mystery and dread.
> Bid, then, the tender light of faith to shine
> By which alone the mortal heart is led
> Unto the thinking of the thought divine.[14]

As I shall attempt to show in the next chapter, this fact of self-transcendence as applied to the understanding of man makes all the difference between a working social faith and a faith that must remain unimplemented. At this point I wish to illustrate the intellectual consequences of a failure to recognize experience as the ultimate locus of religious reality insofar as man can make any approach to it. There is no domain of "reason" except the realm of experience. To assign to rational processes a wholly nonempirical function is to ignore the way in which conceptual systems evolve. The illustration I am choosing is a passage from Professor Micklem's book *What is the Faith?* He has been describing what he recognizes as a common type of allegedly Christian belief, which expresses itself in ethical and non-dogmatic terms—in a word, in humanistic terms. Concerning it he says: "It is a religious position, which, as the fine flowering of Natural Religion, must win respect. I for my part confess that this is all so reasonable, so credible, so close to spiritual realities

[14] George Santayana, *Poems,* Charles Scribner's Sons.

that it is to this position that in my moments of doubt I inevitably revert. This may prove in the end to be the ultimate truth and substance of Christianity, and, indeed, it may be set forth in a form hard to be distinguished from the Christian faith; but essentially it is not the Christian faith and is scarcely a pale reflection of it. I write with feeling here. I did not invent the Christian faith; I learnt it through the Bible and the Church. As a scholar I can define it objectively from the Bible and the Church's Creeds and confessions, whether I believe it or not. My moods vary, my faith flickers; at best I cry, 'Lord, I believe; help Thou mine unbelief.' But in all moods I see clearly the difference between the historic faith of the Church and this modern parody of it which is but the common sense of all religious men."[15]

This was written by a great Christian thinker and leader, whose writings command admiration and respect. It is all the more remarkable, then, that we should find in a book from his pen so striking an illustration of the dilemma into which theologizing may lead. He finds a version of Christianity, which he calls a "parody" of this historic Christian faith, "so reasonable, so credible, so close to spiritual realities" that he reverts to it in his moments of "unbelief." Now my point is not that this "common sense of all religious men" is an

[15] Nathaniel Micklem, *What Is The Faith?* Cokesbury Press, p. 81.

adequate substitute for Christian doctrine; I have insisted that the Christian community must have doctrinal forms that are peculiar to itself, the product of its own corporate life. But the historic body of Christian doctrine is precisely the medium through which the Christian community makes real for itself and relevant to its needs the timeless truths which underlie "the common sense of all religious men." To hold that the supernatural in Christianity consists in a series of particular historic affirmations on which the stoutest faith often loses its grip, rather than in the miracle of the personality of Christ himself, is to substitute an "epic" for a personal, spiritual reality. Is it not reasonable to contend that the conflict between natural and supernatural religion should cease when naturalism divests itself of its mechanistic character and embraces the concept of creative personality? Has it not then within it the essential value that supernaturalism has contended for as against a mechanistic philosophy? At the least, thoughtful consideration should be given to the possibility that much theological ammunition is being fired at a place where an enemy used to be.

The significance of the Christian *mythos* is that it mediates to those reared in the Christian tradition the personality of Christ—a self-authenticating miracle of history. The neo-orthodox writers themselves recognize the difference between the form of the myth and the truth it conveys. Whenever myth is confused with fact endless trouble begins. In every Christian communion there are persons to whom the language of the theologian is alien and who seize on the Christian revelation as embodied in the personality of Christ without benefit of conventional dogma. This is particularly true, it would seem, in the younger churches.

He who has laid hold on the person of Jesus Christ has embraced the totality of the Christian revelation. He knows what sin is because he has seen it through the eyes of his Master. He knows what redemptive love and vicarious suffering mean for he has walked with One who personifies them. By the same token he knows the meaning of the Kingdom of God, for he sees it in a victorious personality who irresistibly confronts a pagan social order and who will never cease to battle with it until it reflects the will of God.

Chapter III

HOW "FALLEN" IS HUMAN NATURE?

AT THE present time the Christian view of man is more in dispute perhaps than any other subject of Christian doctrine. This is, of course, because the current challenge to an activist social ethic is aimed chiefly at assumptions concerning man's capacity for perfectibility. Indeed, the word "perfectibility," in the sense of indefinite improvability, defines the main issue. The question becomes whether or not the nature of man is so heavily weighted with evil—oriented away from God—that only a succession of miraculous happenings, called accessions of grace, can regenerate him. In the orthodox view, grace is an infusion from without and is sharply distinguished from any developmental process. Redemption becomes in this view a punctiliar thing, rather than a continuous process, something in which the voluntaristic element in human life is minimized and in which there is nothing inherently cumulative in the developmental sense. And redemption is so conceived because human nature is held to be so opposed to God that grace is always a stranger in the human heart, never becoming domesticated, so to speak, in man's life.

To be sure, much has been made in evangelical Christianity of the experience of "entire sanctification" but this seems to be as ill at home in the new orthodoxy as it is in liberal Christianity. To the latter it is unrealistic because it abstracts man from the social complex in which he lives—from his social-ethical environment; to the former it is hopelessly romantic perfectionism. In both, it is held suspect because of the highly doubtful quality of its typical exhibits!

The question is this: Is man's religion native to him as man or a conquest of his soul from without? Does man seek God or does God seek him? Or does this antithetic statement present a paradox that is inherent in life itself? Here again I use "paradox" to denote an essential polarity, a dialectic.

Now what is the meaning of this word "dialectic" which is so often used to characterize the new orthodoxy? I think it is an excellent word but one that is easily misused. Dialectic has in it the implication of *process*. The opposites which it presupposes are not mutually exclusive, like the opposites of formal logic. They interpenetrate. One is really implicit in the other. They are related in the process of *becoming*. Now the developmental concept as related to religious and moral experience, which characterizes the liberal Christian view of life and history, is admittedly weak in that it does scant justice to the "crisis" aspect of experience in which man becomes conscious of the opposite poles of his existence. God meets man in challenge, in condemnation: Man becomes aware of himself as a sinner. He cries out, "O wretched man that I am!"

But this very self-awareness is an expression of the tie that binds him in his very nature to God. To say, therefore, that man is incapable of seeking God, of aspiring toward the good, is to deny an elemental fact of human experience.

As I write there comes to my notice an address given some months ago by Professor Homrighausen, an exponent of the new orthodoxy, in which, as it seems to me, he expresses very much the same thought that I am trying to convey. Referring to the objection that supernaturalism leads to dualism, he says: "There is a dualism in the Christian life anyway, a tension, a polarity. Supernatural religion sensitizes man to this dualism, and makes him see life in terms of creative living in the creative tension of life's two dimensions—time and eternity. It takes the nature of life's crises seriously. God and man are not to be divorced, nor are they to be blended into either one or the other."[1] This is one

[1] E. G. Homrighausen, Address Before Professors' Advisory Section of the International Council of Religious Education, Chicago, February, 1939.

more instance of what the current heated theological controversy tends to obscure: the underlying harmony of orthodoxy and liberalism when their real concerns are clarified.

In the view here presented man's religious life tends to be regarded as "natural" to him—that is, belonging to him as man—except in those critical moments when the ethical tension becomes so great that a "block" is experienced in moral effort. Then a theology of crisis intervenes. In other words, the continuity of the religious life—which is another way of saying, its authentic human quality—is precisely a function of the continuity of ethical purpose and action. Now, continuity of experience is something that the mind never fully attains but perpetually strives after. The matter may be put as follows: In the effort to negotiate the external world, man's central concern is to maintain a satisfying equilibrium in which his consciousness is unified. But his world is continually doing things to him which compel him to readjust. The impact of the world upon him is intermittent, varied. This tends continually to give his experience a broken, discrete character. But personal life is precisely man's effort to negotiate the world, to tame it, so to speak, and make it serve his purpose. That purpose is the unifying principle which operates to give order and continuity to human experience. To my mind, this is the essence of a personalist philosophy.

It is interesting to note that Karl Barth seems to recognize this function of religion as something belonging to man, but he puts it aside, insisting that religion is only a threshold to Christianity, which is qualitatively different. The view taken here is, of course, that Christianity is *one* form of religion, and as such, the normative character of its doctrinal structure is limited to the community to which it is indigenous. It is the religion of the Christian community.

Now the tendency to refer religious experience to a source wholly outside man and of a nature opposed to man's nature is due to the need for symbols to express the "critical" aspects of experience—those aspects in which encounter between opposing forces seems to be of the essence. Let us consider the parallel afforded in the ordinary phenomena of consciousness. A man examines *himself*, debates with *himself*, despises *himself*, masters *himself*. Are there then two distinct selves? Is personality dual—or even plural? That question may be answered in the affirmative to the extent that consciousness has always the aspect, not of being unified, but of *becoming* unified, integrated. The inner moral struggle is a contest in which a "better self" strives for mastery. Religiously stated this is precisely the meaning of God in human experience. The better self that is striving for dominance is always transcending what may be called the actual self. In an empirical philosophy, to which the modern mind seems increasingly attached, this transcendence is what makes man human—more than an animal, that puts him in the category of the personal, the creative. Again, in religious terms, the distinctive thing about man is that he is divine, supernatural, if you will, in that he turns back upon nature the full force of his creative will. From an ethical point of view, therefore, the most disastrous thing that a theology can do is to devaluate man. I think it can be shown that the values which the new orthodoxy seeks to conserve are not dependent on a low view of human nature, but will in the end be destroyed by such a view.

All discussion of this question of the nature of man in conventional Protestant terms is difficult. Protestantism does not make much of the distinction found in Catholicism between natural and revealed religion. While everything savoring of "mere humanism" is as distasteful to Catholic as to orthodox Protestant thought, the concepts of natural theology elaborated in Catholic teaching serve to support what may be called normal religious aspiration. It is an important principle of the Scholastic philosophy that revelation, while it runs beyond reason, is never in opposition to it. In the epoch-making synthesis of Aristotle and St.

Augustine which Thomas Aquinas achieved, a link between nature and supernature was established which at least made possible a consistent Christian anthropology and a Christian sociology. I am not, of course, suggesting that the positions I am outlining are acceptable to the Catholic mind, but I believe that the current orthodox trend in Protestant thought is in part due to a lack of insights that Catholic Christianity has possessed from the Middle Ages forward. No Catholic teacher could ever be led into the negative position that eminent Protestants are taking today regarding the relevance of Christianity to the processes of human history. To be sure, the Catholic system of theology ultimately takes on a dualistic pattern. But the break between nature and supernature is not, as in Protestant orthodoxy, so sharp as to prevent the expression of religious motive in an authentic social-ethical program. Witness the deliverances of the Catholic Church on social questions—deliverances which leave no doubt that Christianity, as the Catholic Church conceives it, has a definitely social ethic, and is susceptible of unambiguous formulation in specific terms. The doctrinal difference between the Catholic and the orthodox Protestant view of human nature is thus expressed by a Catholic scholar: "Now, the Catholic-Christian tradition and official theological interpretation of the effects of original sin is decidedly not this dour doctrine of the Genevan reformer. Someone has said that the Catholic doctrine differs from the Calvinist by only a letter but, as in an earlier theological dispute over a letter that shook the Western world, that differing letter indicates a radically different philosophy or life. By reason of Adam's sin, the Calvinist believes that all human nature is *depraved;* therefore, every merely human desire, everything that ministers to human comfort and pleasure is thereby sinful. The Catholic Church, on the contrary, holds that human nature by reason of Adam's sin is *deprived* of certain prerogatives, notably of bodily immortality and perfect control of appetite."[2]

Another Catholic authority puts the matter in more positive terms: "It is native to Catholic Christianity to respect the inherent worth and dignity of human nature. This is not a whim or a fancy. It is of the essence of Catholic theology to recognize that, whatever human nature lost in the loss of original justice, it did not lose its interior integrity as a nature. The Catholic is, by profession, a humanist."[3]

Let us look closely at the paradox in human nature as reflected in orthodox tradition. There is first the concept of man embodied in the great doctrine of *Imago Dei*—man is made in the image of God. Sec-

[2] William J. McGucken, *The Catholic Way in Education*, Bruce Publishing Company, p. 23.

[3] Anton Charles Pegis, in *Education for Democracy*, Teachers College, p. 201.

ondly, there is the doctrine of the fall of man. He is so far removed from God by the action of his perverted will that, as Protestant theology has declared, the divine image is all but obliterated. It may be noted in passing that the "all but" is in effect a vitiating qualification in a theology that would completely exorcise all "humanism." For even here the difference between human and divine is not altogether qualitative. This reservation occurs again and again in orthodox literature and illustrates the ethical inadequacy of a strictly dualistic conception as compared with one that brings contrasting aspects of reality into one framework. The former is transcendentalist in the technical sense; the latter is empirical.

Now the important fact to be noted here for purposes of the present discussion is that historically these conflicting ideas about man are not mutually exclusive. They have functioned correlatively within one Christian community. The Puritans left no device of language unused to put *homo sapiens* beyond defense or mitigation. He has a corrupt nature "whereby he is utterly indisposed, disabled and made opposite to all that is spiritually good, and wholly inclined to all evil, and that continually." All the senses of man, said Jonathan Edwards, "are only inlets and outlets of sin." That is a pretty thorough job of damnation. No Barthian could do better.

But over against this must be put the high dignity of man as the Puritan conceived him. Dr. Maurer has brought these two aspects of Puritan faith into startling juxtaposition, citing Lord Macaulay's characterization, in his essay on Milton, of the Puritan conception of the dignity of man: "The very meanest of them was a being to whose fate a mysterious and terrible importance belonged, on whose slightest action the spirits of light and darkness looked with anxious interest, who had been destined before heaven and earth were created, to enjoy a felicity which should continue when heaven and earth should have passed away. Events which short-sighted politicians ascribed to earthly causes had been ordained on his account. For his sake empires had risen, and flourished, and decayed. . . . He had been ransomed by the sweat of no vulgar agony, by the blood of no earthly sacrifice. It was for him that the sun had been darkened, that the rocks had been rent, that the dead had risen, that all nature had shuddered at the sufferings of her expiring God. Thus the Puritan was made up of two different men, the one all self-abasement, penitence, gratitude, passion; the other proud, calm, inflexible, sagacious. He prostrated himself in the dust before his Maker, but he set his foot on the neck of his king."[4]

Magnificently put. In other words, the Puritan was

[4] Thomas Babington Macaulay, *Milton*, Macmillan Company.

too accomplished a theologian to let his doctrines get in each other's way. To state it more bluntly, he knew how to *use* his doctrines, because he knew to what they were relevant. My contention is that such theological concepts become mischievous when they are held to be absolute. In a normal human situation, by which I mean a situation in which wholesome ethical action is neither blocked nor irrationally accelerated, these concepts function in their right place. It is only in situations conducive to frustration or to neurotic exhilaration that one principle eclipses the other. In frustration man is overwhelmed by his nothingness; under irrational elation, or autointoxication of the spirit, he starts to build a Tower of Babel. Professor Becker cleverly characterizes this extreme as revealed in the nineteenth-century mind. The difference, he says, between eighteenth- and nineteenth-century ideas of progress, "may be expressed, with some exaggeration in the contrast, by saying that whereas the eighteenth century held that man can by taking thought add a cubit to his stature, the nineteenth century held that a cubit would be added to his stature whether he took thought or not."[5]

Neither of these historical doctrines of man, the one affirming his depravity, the other affirming his dignity, is true, even mythologically, when taken out of rela-

[5] Carl L. Becker, "Progress," in *Encyclopedia of the Social Sciences*, Vol. XII, p. 498.

tion to the other. Both are expressions of truth as functions of man's relation to contrary situations. This the Puritans seem to have known right well. Indeed one doctrine supported the other, for man's very meagerness in the sight of God made it irrational that any mortal should lord it over another.

The same conclusion is indicated when we consider the devotional literature of the Old Testament and the doctrinal teaching of St. Paul. Much is made currently of the emphasis placed in the Old Testament on the sin of pride. This is due, of course, to the fact that the burden of prophetic religion is denunciation of the works of man when he has forgotten God. The mood of the psalmists is no more characteristically penitential than it is assured—even self-gratulatory. The burden of their outpourings is now one of contrition as they contemplate the perfection of God, and now one of glorying in the status of security because his will has been done, and his perfection has been appropriated by the obedient heart: "Remember the word unto thy servant, upon which thou hast caused me to hope. This is my comfort in my affliction: for thy word hath quickened me. The proud have had me greatly in derision; yet have I not declined from thy law. I remembered thy judgments of old, O Lord; and have comforted myself."[6] Man in rebellion is indeed an

[6] Psalms 119:49-92.

abased creature, but this is not his true portion: "When I consider thy heavens . . . What is man, that thou art mindful of him? and the son of man, that thou visitest him? For thou hast made him a little lower than the angels, and hast crowned him with glory and honour."[7] And consider the exultation of Paul: "There is therefore now no condemnation to them which are in Christ Jesus, who walk not after the flesh, but after the Spirit. For the law of the Spirit of life in Christ Jesus hath made me free from the law of sin and death."[8] Catholics may well complain that there is an undue—almost morbid—emphasis in Orthodox Protestantism on the depravity of man. To be aware of the abyss does not require that one despair of attaining the heights.

It is a curious fact that current criticism of liberal social Christianity as unrealistic should overlook the strong prophetic note in social gospel literature dealing with collective sin. The followers of Walter Rauschenbusch have had to bear continual reproach from reactionary Christians because they were "running down" man as his works stand revealed in contemporary civilization. Rauschenbusch, Gladden, Strong and Taylor —to mention only a few—would have difficulty in recognizing themselves in current deliverances against

[7] Psalms 8:3-5.
[8] Romans 8:1-2.

what is alleged to be the easy, romantic optimism of the social gospel! For a generation it has been these men and a host of others of kindred mind who have realistically analyzed human life as the tendencies of the human heart are manifested in collective behavior. It has been their critics who insisted that simple, individual conversion was all that was necessary to set the world right. Every preacher of social righteousness has been remonstrated with *ad nauseam* for not trusting entirely in the regeneration of the individual, who is "justified by faith alone." Romanticism might well be charged against these evangelical traditionalists who have never been realistic as they looked at human nature in its collective aspect. Such an accusation is hardly in place when directed at the prophets of the social gospel. Only a sense of the enormity of sin, reinforced by a sense of outrage that human suffering due to man's inhumanity to man should be attributed to an inscrutable divine will, could have motivated the prophetic utterances of the social gospel pioneers. Liberal Christianity is often accused in the words of Anselm: *"Nondum considerasti quanti ponderis sit peccatum."* (Thou hast not considered how great is the weight of sin.) Can anyone believe that true of a man who wrote the following words about sin? "By our very nature we are involved in tragedy. In childhood and youth we have imperious instincts and desires to drive us, and little knowledge to guide and control us. We commit acts of sensuality, cruelty, or dishonor, which nothing can wipe from our memory. A child is drawn into harmful habits which lay the foundation for later failings, and which may trip the man again when his powers begin to fail in later life. How many men and women have rushed with the starry eyes of hope into relations which brought them defilement of soul and the perversion of their most intimate life, but from which they could never again extricate themselves by any wrench. 'Forgive us our trespasses. Lead us not into temptation.' The weakness or the stubbornness of our will and the tempting situations of life combine to weave the tragic web of sin and failure of which we all make experience before we are through with our years." Those are the words of Walter Rauschenbusch.[9] The most thoroughgoing realist is the most authentic herald of a new day.

An evaluation of contrasting views of man must rest on their efficacy in "operational" terms. Preoccupation with his own unworthiness is inevitable when man is confronted by the demands of an absolute ethic. And it is inherent in the Christian ethic that it makes an absolute demand. Here is a point at which confusion often occurs. It is commonly assumed that an experimentalist, activist attitude, in which the criteria of

[9] *Op. cit.*, p. 32.

judgment are relative to emergent situations, precludes recognition of absolutes. Yet a candid examination of the facts should destroy such an assumption. Nothing is more impressive than the propensity of a radical empiricist for absolute judgments. Among all my philosophical acquaintances I know of no idealist who is any more certain of his position, more sure of the correctness of his philosophy than the experimentalists and pragmatists. This is not said in derogation. It is inevitable, because the values of the convinced experimentalist, like those the absolutist seeks to establish, have a mandatory character. So great is the experimentalist's concern for coherence, for relatedness, for continuity in experience that he thunders as from Sinai in their defense. Indeed, all intense ethical experience reveals a quality of absoluteness, for when a person of deep and serious nature has arrived at a moral judgment, no matter by how slow and deliberate a process, that judgment has the same compulsive power as one believed to be derived from a flash of revelation. It is, in other words, quite possible to follow the road of experimental intelligence, so dear to the empiricist, and yet arrive at a moral imperative that has the force of an absolute. As some one has put it, it becomes one's "absolute duty to do his relative best." Stated in these terms the ethical problem of a liberal Christianity is to maintain so earnest a concern for righteousness of life that lack of finality in the content of a moral judgment will not vitiate its absolute character as an immediate imperative.

How then shall the self-assurance which intense belief in man inspires be evaluated? Here, it would seem, the criticism of social Christianity as utopian—and hence demonic, in the technical sense—is sharpest and most challenging. For here, it is earnestly contended, man is engaging in a self-destructive pursuit. He is guilty of the greatest sin, pride. And it is called the greatest sin because it is the surest precursor of a fall. It is quite understandable that the new orthodoxy should see everything "utopian" in this light, even to the high aim of "building the Kingdom of God." A European woman of high Christian character and first-rate mental endowment told me that she had serious doubts about the use of the term "the Kingdom of God" in the statement of purpose of a Christian organization. From her point of view she was right. When the idea of the Kingdom of God is referred to active purpose rather than mere expectancy born of a faith in wholly extraneous forces it makes man definitely a partner in celestial enterprise and invests the historical process itself with real meaning. And this, I contend, is an entirely normal expression of Christian motive in a situation that is not too rigid to admit of effectual effort. But this means that there is true *poten-*

tiality in the human situation. The affirmation of such potentiality I call a fundamental theological postulate. For if merely by virtue of a great hope and an effort to organize his life around it man is fooling himself because he does not know himself his last state can only be worse than his first.

Now, it must be admitted that disillusionment about man and his enterprises is too characteristic of the current mood to be lightly put aside. There are expressions of it that reflect significant insights.

The essential point here, as in the understanding of the Psalms, would seem to be the distinction between pride and confidence. Pride is based on an erroneous assumption about one's status. All pride is "false pride." It is the sin of him who only *thinketh* he standeth. Confidence of spiritual potency grows out of an authentic sense of the dignity of man's nature. He *can* because of what he *is*—a child of God. Let us look at some of the negative testimony concerning the significance of human instrumentality implied in contemporary judgments about the state of the world. President Seymour of Yale has said about the present period: "Never in the history of the world has the menace of materialism been more appalling nor the disastrous consequences of its triumph so obvious. In the political, economic and social fields of endeavor it has produced and it will perpetuate suicidal strife." And President Butler of

Columbia says that we live in "a world facing the gravest crisis which has confronted it in more than a thousand years." The Oxford Conference of 1937 declared that today "as probably only once or twice before in human history, the foundations themselves are shaken." These expressions of mood, all antedating the present war, while perhaps not wholly typical, at least reflect a trend toward crisis thinking, one that finds support in current diagnoses of the economic and political situation which point to the conclusion that epochal changes are upon us.[10]

Now, the important thing to be noted about such judgments is that they are rendered alike by people who make them the basis of despair and those who find in them a challenge to greater effort. We may note, for example, how Nicolas Berdyaev gives free rein to his pessimism with reference to the collapse of human hope and enterprise. "Man's historical experience has been one of steady failure and there are no grounds for supposing that it will ever be anything else. Not one single project elaborated within the historical process has ever proved successful. . . ."[11] In contrast notice the way in which a social activist faces the threatened defeat of idealistic purposes. In the concluding passage of his *Liberalism and Social Action* John Dewey says:

[10] The quotations from President Seymour and President Butler are from newspaper reports of academic addresses.

[11] *The Meaning of History,* Charles Scribner's Sons, p. 198.

[99]

"It may be that the way will remain untrodden. If so, the future holds the menace of confusion moving into chaos, a chaos that will be externally masked for a time by an organization of force, coercive and violent, in which the liberties of men will all but disappear. Even so, the cause of the liberty of the human spirit, the cause of opportunity of human beings for full development of their powers, the cause for which liberalism enduringly stands, is too precious and too ingrained in the human constitution to be forever obscured. . . . The business of liberalism is to bend every energy and exhibit every courage so that these precious goods may not even be temporarily lost but be intensified and expanded here and now."[11a]

What a contrast! The orthodox theologian is as pessimistic about the whole world as Spengler is about the West, or as a moody physicist pondering the second law of thermodynamics and the gradual running down of the universe. The "humanist," on the other hand, affirms undying faith in a spiritual destiny which the human race is not to be denied.

The point here is that the dominance of one such attitude over another reflects the situational background of beliefs. To be sure, a superficial optimism about civilization is less intellectually and morally respectable than a pessimism that grows out of sober regard for realities. To tell a person who sees only foreboding in

[11a] G. P. Putnam's Sons, p. 93.

the current scene that people have felt that way again and again—and to document it, as we might do—is not convincing to him. In a world which presents real novelty, as both transcendental and naturalistic theism hold, the possibility of tragic failure cannot be excluded. Only a crude providentialism, as distasteful to the neo-orthodox as to the liberal mind, can give warrant for an easy optimism about the world. To any but a naïve mind tragedy is real and is inherent in life. I believe, therefore, that the possibility of an impending dark age must be seriously entertained as we look ahead. The question is, what does a realistic attitude toward life do to religious faith concerning human destiny?

Here we come to grips with the question whether what we know about man gives warrant for the con-clusion which the new orthodoxy reaches that human instrumentality operating within the historical process is not a positive resource. In a word, what is a tenable view of human nature? To answer the question we must consider the testimony of science as it bears on the significance of man's ethical purposes and his social aims. For as already stated, the issue is whether or not there is *true potentiality* in the human situation. For the validity of the social gospel can be defended only by reference to what we know about man. If there were any question about the pertinence of scientific testi-mony it should be disposed of by noting that the newer orthodoxy in sustaining its emphasis on the *im*perfect-ibility of human nature appeals directly to historical evidence of the part played by greed and pride in human life. The appeal for "realism" in theology has exactly this import.

Now, it must be frankly avowed that the testimony of biology gives much support to the view that human perfectibility is an idle dream. Biological science sees man as the product of an evolutionary process that has continued through millions of years. Even the very small segment of geological time during which man has lived on the earth is probably not less than half a million years. Hence every human being is born with a biological inheritance which is so firmly estab-lished that anything that may happen within the life history of the individual tending to change his original nature is insignificant by comparison. Furthermore, the very mechanism of inheritance seems to exclude the possibility that acquired characters may be transmitted to offspring. In other words, it is impossible for man "by taking thought" to add one cubit to his biological stature. Original human nature—the capacities and tendencies that one is born with—remains almost con-stant from one millennium to another. I say "almost" because biologists today recognize that "gene muta-tions" do occur and that even original human nature may be altered by small increments. There is no reason, however, to assume that these occur in any pre-established direction. So far as we know they are wholly fortuitous. And in any case, to have cumulative importance they would have to continue over such long periods as to dwarf all historical reckoning.

Not only so, but man has so taken himself in hand, collectively, that the working of natural selection through struggle for survival has been virtually superseded by what we may call cultural selection. Civilized man deliberately rescues the biologically handicapped from the extinction to which nature would condemn them. It is one of the paradoxes of history that social evolution through the operation of ethical forces should have turned back sharply on the mechanisms of biological evolution to nullify their operation. We subsidize, as it were, the physically unfit, hospitalize the mentally unfit and give a large measure of social support to the morally inferior. A congenital handicap that in the state of nature would spell doom is made the occasion for an expression of the humane spirit which is forever gainsaying the urge of nature to purify the stream of inheritance. The net result is that in man little elimination from the stream of inheritance because of biological inferiority actually takes place. Man has in no small measure usurped the place of nature in the control of inheritance by putting an end to the struggle for physical survival. His very humanitarianism has nullified his biological advance.

To many, the inference to be drawn from these facts is that sex selection should be rationalized by the application of a eugenic formula. They maintain that the biologically "given" in human inheritance makes permanent improvement of human life a hopeless task except as this inheritance is dealt with in a rational way. Some eugenicists would solve the problem by "Burbanking" the human race. If man can by simple breeding make super-racehorses, why not supermen? But the difficulties in such a program are too great in the present state of our knowledge about inheritance to admit of scientific procedures even if we were willing to experiment on the human race on so vast a scale. That education as it affects sex selection among men and women accomplishes actual improvement in the human stock may be taken for granted. But the process is chiefly a negative one, accomplishing elimination of morbid inheritance, such as gross emotional instability, and even that only in limited degree. We are not even agreed on what the most desirable mental traits are, and if we were, there is so much in the inheritance of the individual that is recessive (concealed, and discoverable only in the offspring) that the imagination falters before the task of making over humanity by a biological process. We seem to be rather sharply limited to procedures that take man, biologically, as he is.

It may be noted here that the several types of analytic psychology, which put great stress on the "unconscious" as the repository of irrational inherited drives, contributes much to the "contemporary devaluation of man." No more telling attack upon social idealisms can be made by the most ardent Augustinian theologian than by a Freudian psychologist. Stored up in the Id are all the tendencies that man's animal inheritance has contributed to the determination of his destiny. This reservoir of unrecognized tendencies is continually overflowing into conscious life. Once the controls of civilized living give way man appears as the "old savage," driven by primitive urges and setting at naught the restraints of law and custom. This is why long years of effort to eradicate lynching or to "civilize" war or to humanize industrial relations seem to go for nothing when the dikes against primitive passion give way. The current orthodox emphasis on original sin has scientific support to the extent that psychology of the analytic type gives a true picture of psychic inheritance.

The net result of consulting biology and the forms of psychology that are in high degree biologically oriented is that man has a permanent inheritance that makes him capable of the most bestial conduct. There is no known way to eradicate that sinister aspect of human nature from man's animal inheritance. The potentiality of evil remains. The orthodox theologians score. If we had nothing more to guide us in the testimony of science than these evidences we might well conclude that an unrelieved account of the corruption of man's nature through a fall from grace is a tolerably acceptable mythical account of man as we know him.

But we have not yet put our question to the cultural anthropologist. It is here that we find an entirely different kind of testimony. Studies of human culture are, of course, limited by the fact that there exists nothing that is wholly "primitive"; we have only approximations to original types of human association. But enough is known to make fairly certain the conclusion that culture is highly selective in character with reference to possible patterns of behavior. Observation of peoples approximating the same stage of development proves that a wide range of attitudes and tendencies exists in relation to interests and propensities which were formerly thought to be standardized throughout the human race. We find warlike attitudes and peaceable attitudes; competitive behavior and co-operative behavior; exploitive sex patterns and socialized sex patterns; men who perform social functions and display attitudes commonly supposed to belong to women, and vice versa.

Margaret Mead in one of her important anthropological studies has given an impressive illustration of the fallacy so common among us that our civilization is an expression of human nature in some fixed and final sense. "To the Arapesh," she writes, "the world is a garden that must be tilled, not for one's self, not in pride and boasting, not for hoarding and usury, but that the yams and the dogs and the pigs and most of all the children may grow. From this whole attitude flow many of the other Arapesh traits, the lack of conflict between old and young, the lack of any expectation of jealousy or envy, the emphasis upon cooperation. Cooperation is easy when all are whole-heartedly committed to a common project from which no one of the participators will himself benefit. Their dominant conception of men and women may be said to be that of regarding men, even as we regard women, as gently, carefully parental in their aims."[12]

Indeed, it is difficult to name any kind of behavior, except for very simple unlearned reactions, which may be pronounced "instinctive" in the older sense of that word. In every culture the animal inheritance of man is always found operating, but *it is culture patterns that select among native capacities those that shall be given right of way*. It is as if life were a stream coming down from mountain sources and making its way through

[12] *Sex and Temperament in Three Primitive Societies,* p. 135 and *Sex and Temperament* in *From the South Seas,* William Morrow Company.

lowlands to the open sea. It is bound to flow, but there are any number of possible channels through which it may take its journey.

The most astonishing thing about human nature is its repertoire of possible responses to situations. Man is capable of almost infinite variety in the patterns of behavior which may become effective controls in his culture.

In short, the quest for *original* human nature which interested psychologists so much a few years ago is seen to be much less significant than the study of the various forms of *developed* human nature which cultural anthropology discloses. The similarity observed in human behavior over the face of the earth is striking, to be sure, but definite cultural correspondence extends only to those traits that become universalized through community of environmental influence. There is no reason to suppose that any culture which provides for elemental human needs may not by the process of cultural selection fix any one of a huge variety of sharply contrasting patterns of individual behavior. Man needs food, clothing, shelter, love, work, adventure, art, religion; but among the wide variety of ways in which these wants may be satisfied methods so different may be developed as to make one marvel that the contrasted societies come from a common biological source.

Now the significance of this for our inquiry should be at once apparent, but the point in stressing it is that it seems to be generally overlooked. If we were making such an inquiry as educators or social scientists we should be driven inescapably to the conclusion that the one hope of human betterment is in nobly motivated cultural change. We should have at once a charter for social education on a grand scale under the inspiration of high religion. But where the new deflationary religious mood prevails, a theological approach to the same problem leads to a conclusion that spells moral defeatism. I repeat that all we have any right to ask for is assurance that indefinite perfectibility is not excluded as we address ourselves to the modification of human nature. And this the evidence gives us a warrant for accepting as a working faith. By a curious twist of thinking the newer orthodoxy passes over from the concept of *perfectibility* to *perfectionism*, and assumes that one who affirms the former is embarked upon the adventure of becoming God! As already remarked, evangelicalism with its emphasis on holiness as a state attainable in the midst of an unholy world was romantic in the extreme, but it was precisely against that form of ethical romanticism that the social gospel made its protest. Not arrival at a goal, but validated progress in the direction of it, gives life its zest and faith its warrant.

It is, then, in the very facts about human imperfection which the new orthodoxy makes so much of that liberal social Christianity finds a compulsion toward what it calls "Kingdom building." It makes a deliberate adaptation of a gospel originally cast in an apocalyptic framework in order to render more authentically for a changed historical situation its message of human redemption. For liberal Christianity can see no necessary connection whatever between the absolute ethic of Jesus and the particular apocalyptic framework in which it was presented. The timeless truth must be lifted out of a setting that definitely *dated* it and made relevant to a world to which apocalyptic thinking is alien.

In this connection we should consider the significance of utopian conceptions. It is the fashion among orthodox writers today to put all melioristic theories and efforts in one category and classify them as "utopian"— hence humanistic and demonic. Now the word "demonic" is a useful one in that it denotes the insidiousness of all worship of half-gods. It signifies the apotheosis of the partial, the fragmentary, good, the attribution of a spurious adequacy to the inadequate. It is this that is so tragically illustrated in the current demonism of state worship. But this is no warrant for consigning all utopias to the demonic category. Rightly understood, utopia is an ethical construct, the "inverted myth" to which reference was made earlier. There is a sense in which ethics is opposite to religion—that is, to religion in the prophetic sense. For prophetic religion takes the standpoint of God. It views man, so to speak, as God sees him. Ethics takes man, resting under this terrible judgment, and undertakes to do something about him. In this prophetic sense religion looks downward, taking the standpoint of God, while ethics looks up, taking the standpoint of man. It was a synthesis of these points of view that we saw operating in the Puritan consciousness. But it is a synthesis that can be held only under the aspect of rhythm. Man sits under judgment, then rises to vindicate his moral will. Utopia is thus a dynamic ethical concept, impelling man forward from the imperfection that *is* toward the perfection that he feels a moral imperative to seek. This distinction should, I think, resolve in part at least the conflict between the orthodoxy of our time and the liberal Christianity which it so severely criticizes.

Mannheim in his able work *Ideology and Utopia* presents an illuminating contrast between deceptive illusions that destroy ethical validity and the work of creative imagination that reacts upon things as they are. The former he calls "ideologies," the latter "utopias." Both terms apply to ideas that are "situationally transcendent." Ideology seeks a conceptual restructuring of the situation to fit the realities. Says Mannheim:

"The idea of Christian brotherly love, for instance, in a society founded on serfdom remains an unrealizable and, in this sense, ideological idea, even when the intended meaning is, in good faith, a motive in the conduct of the individual. To live consistently, in the light of Christian brotherly love, in a society which is not organized on the same principle is impossible. The individual in his personal conduct is always compelled —in so far as he does not resort to breaking up the existing social structure—to fall short of his own nobler motives."[13] It is the natural tendency of ideology, thus defined, to substitute fantasy for reality and to make a false, ineffectual and ignoble adjustment to life. "As for utopias, they too," says Mannheim, "transcend the social situation, for they too orient conduct towards elements which the situation, in so far as it is realized at the time, does not contain. But they are not ideologies, i.e. they are not ideologies in the measure and in so far as they succeed through counteractivity in transforming the existing historical reality into one more in accord with their own conceptions."[14] Thus the utopia may be constructively dynamic, whereas the ideology is an instrument of reaction.

This distinction, it seems to me, is of prime importance because of the curious aberration that leads to putting social utopias in the same category with those

[13] Karl Mannheim, *Ideology and Utopia*, Harcourt, Brace and Company, p. 175.
[14] *Ibid.*, p. 176.

ideologies which enthrone the political State or an
economic class. The social utopia exalts man by projecting him into the infinite, into the realm of perfection. It fosters imagination that runs beyond factual
expectation. The current totalitarian ideologies in so
far as they fragmentize humanity are antihumanistic.
They do not exalt man but degrade him. They subordinate the personal spirit in the interest of an abstraction. Religious utopias exalt the human by projecting it
Godward.

The central truth here is that a faith which links
man in an essential way with the purposes that he
believes to be underwritten, as it were, in a universe of
which he is a part can energize him as nothing else
can. The error which the intuitions of religion have
always found in humanism is its preoccupation with
intellectual effort, with scientific devices and material
fabrications, rather than with the spiritual creativity
with which man as a person is endowed. This error is
symbolized in the Promethean myth in which the
"titanic" exerts itself in violation of the spiritual. The
contrasting idea is expressed superlatively well in the
redemption chorus of the angels at the culmination of
Goethe's Faust:

> Saved is this noble soul from ill,
> Our spirit-peer. Whoever
> Strives forward with unswerving will,
> Him can we aye deliver.

The utopian concept points to the true function of ethical idealism. Certainly the orthodox theologian who announces with all solemnity that man fell from grace or that God made of one blood all the races of men, knowing full well that he is speaking in mythological terms, should not criticize the Christian liberal who lifts his eyes from crass reality to a far-distant ideal and cries "These things shall be!" All religious truth transcends historic time but it loses ethical meaning whenever it is divorced from the historical process.

Man, then, in contrast to all we know of the lower orders of life, is in his nature self-transcending. That is what it means to say that man is a moral being. Likewise when we say that man is religious we are really saying that he is able to rise above himself and look down upon himself in a judgment that partakes of the judgment of God—that is, it views human nature from the standpoint of the absolute. Under the command, "Be ye perfect," men still fail to be perfect, but they understand what it means. "He hath set eternity in their heart."

An important aspect of the problem of human nature is the relative moral level of individual and group, of man and society. Probably nothing in the current devaluation of human nature is so damaging to the social gospel as the insistence that society is *necessarily* less moral than man. The social gospel centers in the proposition that the further realization of the ideal of love in human relations waits upon its further incorporation in the social structure itself. If man in his corporate relations is necessarily on a lower level than man in his solitude then the Christian social hope is illusory. Society, by its very nature, affords the means of implementing the highest insights of its more sensitive souls. Except as these insights are given support in the social structure they evaporate and the discerning individual falls back in disillusionment. Even intelligent rescue mission work recognizes that only in social support can the power of high resolution be sustained. This is also the philosophy underlying all social legislation. It is an implementation of ideals that can be individually conceived but can only be socially effectuated.

Much has been made of Professor Whitehead's statement that religion is what man does with his solitariness. If you have never been solitary, he says, you have never been religious. One feels intuitively that this is in a significant sense true. But it seems to run so far counter to all that is known about religion in relation to group purposes and group striving that one is given pause in accepting it. May it not be that here again we are dealing with essential paradox? Mounier has an impressive passage on what he calls the "sentiment of solitude." It is, he says, "the consciousness of the entire

[115]

unspiritualized and therefore unpersonalized margin of my interior life and of my exterior relations."[15] Thus solitude becomes not an alternative to community but a technique for increasing one's capacity for experiencing community.

Mysticism illuminates this problem of transcendence by bringing it within a framework of religious experience. The mystic *experiences*; he does not *rationally know*. Because of his insistence that he experiences God the current theological mood discredits him. This is because mystical union implies identity of substance and the current orthodoxy makes no place for that. Now the significant thing about the mystic's experience is not its knowledge content: it is no substitute for reason or for scientific observation. The significant thing in it is its quality of transcendence which reveals how small a part of humanity is comprehended in "man as he is." The fallacy of the concept of "mere man" is made apparent in some striking sentences of Rufus Jones in *The Testimony of the Soul*. "It seems to me," he says, "that *transcendence* belongs inherently to the full meaning of a personal spirit. The complete nature of a person could never be *found* by adding the sum of its past experiences, nor could its next stage of experience ever be predicted by summations of the past. There is always a *beyond* which cannot quite be

[15] *Op. cit.*, p. 99.

accounted for in terms of calculation. We can never say, 'I am.' There is 'more' which must be waited for. 'We partly are and wholly hope to be.' It is impossible to make *immanence* intelligible without *transcendence*, even in the case of our own personal spirits."[16]

Here again my argument finds support in a passage from a foremost exponent of the neo-orthodox position. "Man," says Emil Brunner, "is not merely what he is; his peculiar being is characterized by that inward and higher 'something' which confronts him either with a challenge or at least with pressure from without. But this element which confronts him does so as that which is 'over against' him, and not as an 'object.' It is genuinely 'over against' him, whereas objects are not really 'over against' but 'beneath' us. This challenge, then, is not foreign to man's life, but it comes as a call to one's own nature, as the call to accept responsibility for one's own life, to be truly oneself, and yet it exercises a kind of compulsion. Man is not only one who can ask questions because he is subject; but he is one who *must* ask them—one who is constrained to do so because he does not yet know, and is not yet what he would be. Whether he will or not, in some way or other he must reach out beyond himself; he must transcend himself; he must measure his thinking, willing, and acting by something higher than himself."[17]

[16] Macmillan Company, page 110.
[17] *Man in Revolt*, tr. Olive Wyon, Charles Scribner's Sons, pp. 19-20.

What this comes to, as I see it, is that personality itself embraces the creative power which the word "supernatural" has been used to designate. In such a view there is no need to go outside experience, for religious experience in its nature embraces God. That is what it means, at the highest level, to be a person. The stupendousness of the fact of personality is coming to be appreciated today much more adequately than Protestant orthodoxy has made possible. *"A person,"* says Mounier, *"is a spiritual being, constituted as such by its manner of existence and independence of being; it maintains this existence by its adhesion to a hierarchy of values that it has freely adopted, assimilated, and lived by its own responsible activity and by a constant interior development; thus it unifies all its activity in freedom and by means of creative acts develops the individuality of its vocation."*[18]

In a world where ethical purpose has a reasonable chance to function Christianity expresses itself in confident activity aimed at effecting a nearer approximation to the ideal in human relationships. Overwhelming preoccupation with human unworth is normative only, if one may so use words, in an abnormal situation. Purposeful action leaves little room for self-contemplation. The less time a man has to think upon himself the less likely he will be to think too highly of himself!

[18] *Op. cit.,* p. 68.

Nothing is so well calculated to preserve a true perspective on the human situation as absorption in worthy effort—in the business of being a person. An affirmative attitude toward the world makes for vigorous realism. Where did the idea come from that the prophets of the social gospel have been romantic dreamers? It seems much truer to say that "the proclaimers of the gospel of 'the fatherhood of God and the brotherhood of man' have in the main been . . . men who faced the full brunt of the real world in all its apparent and manifest harshness and sternness, but maintained their conviction unshaken that the deeper reality was other than this."[19]

It is because I believe so strongly that the purpose of theology is to activate Christian living that I doubt the power of any theological system to endure that does not inspire a great purpose undergirded by a great hope. It will avail little in the modern world to construct elaborate systems of thought if people go away from church or classroom saying, "I find no sufficient warrant for making the great effort that it will take to change the world." In their moments of quiet and reflection, in their effort to negotiate the stubborn inexorable aspects of existence men will continue to be overawed in their feebleness by the majesty of God.

[19] A. B. Brown and J. W. Harvey, *The Naturalness of Religion,* James Clarke and Company, p. 72.

There let them purge themselves of whatever demonic pride they have been guilty of. But in the world of action they need all the sense of dignity they can muster. If moralistic pride is the worst of sins, moral paralysis is the worst of misfortunes.

Chapter IV

THE DIVINE SOCIETY

THE Church is the visible embodiment of Christianity as a social experience. It is the "beloved community" sustained by the personality of its Founder. This is to my mind the most important thing that can be said about it. But that simple statement is profoundly theological. It expresses a relationship between human beings under the aspect of their essential divinity—a relationship that is timeless, as creeds and rituals are not. It is a conspicuous lack in American Christianity that the Church remains so vague a concept. There is no clear idea among us as to what the nature of the Church is or as to the criteria by which its functions may be determined. To be sure, there is an extensive literature on the subject, but much of it is—to employ again the terms of the main argument running through this series—not relevant to the existing situation. In any case few Americans, ministers or laymen read it.

It will be recognized at once that current discussion of the Christian social message and of ways in which it can be implemented in action involves conflicting theories of what the Church is and how it stands related to the world. For our purposes it will be sufficient at this point to note the general character of contending theories of the Church without going into finer distinctions that are made by theologians in the various Christian bodies.

To begin with we may note that the conflicting views have, broadly speaking, two aspects, one theological in the strict interpretation of that term, the other sociological. When a question is raised concerning the nature of the Church as the corporate embodiment of a religious testimony the reference is specifically theological; when, on the other hand, the question concerns the life of the Church as a society of persons within a larger community, the reference is sociological. This distinction is recognized alike by orthodox and liberal writers. Thus the theologians at ecumenical conferences characterize the Church as a divine institution, but as one having its roots in the world and so having a "sin-infected" character. Most liberal writers, on the other hand, while preoccupied with the Church as a society of believers, are also concerned to maintain a concept that will express its unique, permanent, witness-bearing character. The theological and sociological elements of the problem are closely interrelated.

The traditional view in Protestantism, as in Catholicism, is that the Church is a *given*, divinely instituted, in contradistinction from all those aspects of human life which may be said to have "evolved." It comes down from God, as a divine intrusion in history. In this traditional view the Church is clearly supernatural, in the interventionist sense, and its authority is *sui generis*. During the past two centuries, however, a number of influences have been at work that have done violence to the traditional doctrine. The impact of modern science, of the philosophy of the Enlightenment, of the study of religious origins, and of the historical criticism of the Bible has done much to undermine this traditional view and to reorient Christian thought concerning the Church. Particularly, the theological trend associated with the names of Schleiermacher, Ritschl, Harnack and Troeltsch identified the Church with the history of a religious community, and concentrated attention upon it as a social phenomenon. It is, of course, no accident that liberal social Christianity, on its theological side, stems from the movement they represented. The redirection of thought about the Church was all of a piece with changed emphases in the Christian message itself.

Now, the current orthodox revival in Europe developed definitely vis-à-vis this liberal theological movement. It is a reaction against that movement, as its literature plainly shows. Christian liberalism is the particular object at which it tilts. The revival of transcendentalist emphasis in respect to the Church is, if my thesis is correct, subject to the generalizations that were offered earlier concerning man's thought of the nature of God. Recent developments in the world—the creation of a new historical situation—made such conceptual adaptations inevitable.

It would be an oversimplification, however, to regard this conflict in the dogmatic realm as due entirely to secular influences. It was in no small part the delayed result of the Protestant Reformation itself. The shattering effect of the Reformation on the whole institutional structure that was built up in the Middle Ages will be considered at some length in the chapter which follows. It should be noted here, however, that in pre-Reformation times all phases of life were informed with common spiritual assumptions—assumptions which have in modern times found no permanent support in the secular world. Indeed, the present concern for an ecumenical Christianity has implicit in it a tribute to the unifying principle that ruled the civilized world before the fragmentizing of religious and political life that came with the waning of the Holy Roman Empire and the rise of the national states. But it is difficult to imagine any combination of circumstances that could have prevented a gradual change in the doctrine of the Church, once the full implications of this fragmentizing process had come to be felt. Whatever the fortunes of the newly energized ecumenical drive—and it had large possibilities before the outbreak of war—it is hardly likely to succeed in establishing a high degree of uniformity in the doctrine of the Church. Indeed, it is a difficulty inherent in the current ecumenical movement that it is not ready to avow such an ideal of uniformity of belief as would make possible the maintenance of the traditional view of the Church. To a significant degree the movement is burdened by an inner contradiction. It clings to a view of the Church the logic of which requires a degree of organic unity which the movement has enough social realism to reject as impractical.

The complexity of the problem increases with analysis. What is the relation between the Church and the individual Christian? It is part and parcel of the traditional view that the divine community which is the Church is prior, logically speaking, to the individual. One belongs to it not by voluntary choice, for ideally he is born and reared in it. His status as an individual Christian is derived from his membership in the Church. The doctrine that salvation comes through the Church is to be understood in the sense of the priority of the Christian community. As such it is a highly significant doctrine, and profoundly social.

The traditional view derives, of course, from the

fact that the Church from the fourth century on was a communal institution in the sense that it had its roots in the community itself. It was one of two societies, the other being the State, into which a person came at birth, and to which he belonged by virtue of merely existing. That was a splendid conception. It made the religious phase of life a primary thing. It was no more an "elective" aspect of experience than was political citizenship. The idea is reminiscent of the social philosophy of the ancient Greeks and the ancient Hebrews with whom religion and politics were never separate. Incidentally, it is against this background of Catholic philosophy that all current efforts of the Roman Church to assert the primacy of spiritual authority must be appraised. In a nation like ours Catholic political attitudes are held suspect by the Protestant majority as manifestations of sectarian aggression. To the Catholic himself these attitudes are the inevitable reaction of a religion that is historically communal and inclusive to a civilization that is predominantly secular.

Now, this conception of the Church as communal and prior to the individual is something that the current orthodox revival seeks to recover. It sees clearly that the Church in liberal Christianity has become something quite different from that, in respect to the character of the membership relation. On the Continent one hears the criticism of such churchmanship as is common in

America that it is a purely voluntary matter, and hence casual. "You join your church as you do your club. The Church cannot be so regarded. Membership in it is rather of the nature of membership in a family. You may, to be sure, desert your family, but you cannot resign from it at will." Here we see the communal principle asserting itself. The Church in this view takes on the nature of an "order" of creation except that it is superior to all other orders—family, community or racial group. The communal Church here confronts the "gathered" Church—the voluntary society of believers. The latter conception is predominant in America.

The conflict between the two conceptions is fundamental, though not irresolvable. The communal principle is deeply established in Catholic Christianity and in theory is an authentic part of Protestant doctrine. The Reformers seem to have had no intention of changing in any fundamental way the doctrine of the Church.

But the "gathered" Church, too, is a true Protestant child, for only by maintaining the ecclesiastical validity of a voluntary religious fellowship could the Reformation Church exist.

Here is revealed a paradox in orthodox Protestantism itself—the doctrine of the Church as a divine society, a body of original spiritual jurisdiction, if one may coin the phrase, is maintained along with the strongly individualist doctrine of the universal priesthood of believers! The former creates a perpetual nostalgia for the Church as Catholicism knows it; the latter breeds sectarianism at high speed.

This conflict was amusingly illustrated for me in a conversation some years ago with a venerable Lutheran friend, a stalwart churchman and citizen whose name had been written large in the service of his community. He had commented on the way in which Christianity transcends all ecclesiastical boundaries, and I said to him, "But Luther said that a man who would find Christ must first find the Church." "Oh, yes," he replied, "I've said that, too, but it isn't true!" The informing genius of Protestantism is a sort of dual personality. It insists that somehow the individual must stand alone before God; yet it continually reaffirms the uniquely divine nature of the Church as a vehicle of grace. These emphases, moreover, are derived in undoubtedly authentic fashion from the Hebrew-Christian tradition, in which we find continual alternation of emphasis on the primacy of the individual and on the priority of the religious community. It would seem that we have here a paradox that cannot be easily disposed of. It is my contention that this paradox is inherent in life itself; it is of a piece with that polarity, to which we referred earlier, that characterizes all human effort to realize spiritual values. Any adequate organization of religious life must produce a more authentic individuality; but this can result only in vital community.

We find the issue accentuated in sectarian Christianity wherever nascent religious energies are at work. For the very prevalence in Protestantism of the idea of justification by faith endows the individual with freedom to make his own alliances. The resulting emergence of religious movements evidences the prolific character of Protestantism. Yet, as a friend of mine has said, a sect requires "a great deal of heat to hatch it out," and this energy develops new and compact religious communities. It is in the small sects that the authority of a special group discipline over life is most strongly emphasized. We have here a situation that seems to cut across the ecumenical premise, for the more churches there are, the more they are the Church!

The saving feature in this religious picture is the fact that the affirmation of religious authority as residing in the sectarian group is subject in no small measure to the influence of general intelligence, and sooner or later it becomes obvious to the sectarian mind that the authority it recognizes is after all relevant to the community which acknowledges it. That is to say, the Church in an authoritative sense is not and cannot be universal. The universal Church can only be a fellowship of churches whose members employ their own particular insights but who can find immeasurable spiritual support in common counsel and in the continual cross-fertilization of thought and experience. These are the values that are expressed in the urge on the part of the smaller bodies on the liberal edge of Protestantism to be included in the ecumenical movement. They have no willingness to surrender the independence of their group testimony, and the traditional view of the Church is quite unacceptable to them, but they feel none the less the authentic appeal of *Una Sancta*.

All of which leads to the conclusion, as I believe, that the key to the nature of the Church is to be found in the spiritual principle of community—the shared experience of those who are participating in an effort to realize in their common life the lordship of Jesus. It is here, if at all, that the concept of the Church can be rehabilitated in an intellectual milieu that admits of no concept of absolute institutional authority. And it is here, I think, that we shall find the clue to the social function of the Church. For myself, I must reject in toto any theory of that social function which does not spring inevitably from the nature of the Church itself. Liberal Christianity has tended to put the Church busy at whatever good work needs to be done. This recourse to a general principle of social utility makes the Church indistinguishable from secular agencies.

Now the principle of community is one that has been

but little explored. The word has many significations, but running through them all is the property of human association by virtue of which it tends to develop the individual in some phase of his life. One person may, and normally does, have membership in many communities. He may be, for example, a member of a church, a labor union and a consumers' cooperative. Each is qualitatively different and yet each has an inclusive character in the sense that one tends to live his life, in each one of the aspects represented, within these respective fellowships. They are distinct, but not mutually exclusive. Within limits one's loyalty to each may be stronger because of his loyalty to the others. The experience mediated through one is in some degree reflected in the others.

It will be said at once that these three illustrations do not belong in the same series, that the Church is *sui generis*. It is, in truth, but so are the others. The distinctive thing about the Church is that it is the community in which men share the process of total evaluation of every aspect of life, arrive at what they conceive to be a spiritual judgment on their own lives in the light of an absolute imperative, formulate corporate ethical standards for their governance, and unify the entire experience in corporate worship. In all these communities the principle of authority is recognized, for that principle is precisely the superiority of group thinking, group aspiration, and group testing of values, in a shared experience of personal discipleship carried on against a background of a rich tradition—the superiority of this group life over anything the individual can achieve in isolation. And the fact which attests the authority of the religious community is the stimulus given to what I have called the self-transcending process —the religious experience *par excellence*—by fellowship of inquiry and of striving. What else can be the significance of that great charter of Christian community, "Where two or three are gathered together in my name, there am I"? Community is not an *additive* concept. It is not a sum-total. It is a distinctive *somewhat* in the nature of human association. The genius of Christianity has always been bound up with the reality of the Christian community, though its creative character has often been overlaid and stifled by artificial purposes and defense reactions. Christian conversion has characteristically meant adoption into a Christian brotherhood.

If this is true, Christianity today is weak because the life-generating force of community is so limited in operation. Wherever anything vital is going on in the religious world it expresses itself in the creation or the revitalizing of groups. The key to this is in creative spiritual sharing. It is this principle, I think, and not the notion of private divine guidance, that gives vigor to the Oxford Group Movement. It is what makes

Christian Science so rewarding to those who belong to its compact fellowship. It is what put Methodism on the religious map of the world. It is not merely a matter of sharing what people already have: it is a sharing of a creative experience that could not happen in isolation. The Christian sacrament of the Lord's Supper originated, it is believed, in a common meal, a sort of basket supper. It began in a tangible sharing of physical food. It became a sacrament as this food became a symbol of an invisible sharing in spiritual rebirth.

I am putting forward the view that the Christian message for the world is a message which comes down from the past only in the sense that the community which authenticates it has its roots in the past. " 'Back to Christ,' " says Canon Barry, "is an inspiring cry: but in fact we can only find Him if we go where His people are. If it means Back to the Synoptic Gospels, at least half their meaning evaporates—some would say that they become meaningless—if we ignore that common experience which they assume and from which they come. They were born out of the worshipping community. . . . The Christian redemption of the social order is offered the world through this redeemed society."[1]

To write in this vein is to make a personal confession of error, even to cry "Peccavi," which I sincerely do. For years I sought to promulgate the Christian social

[1] F. R. Barry, *The Relevance of the Church*, Charles Scribner's Sons, p. 59.

[133]

faith as something definitely formulated that must be preached *at* the Church whether people were prepared to receive it or not. I thought that there was some self-operating principle about social prophecy which would vindicate itself no matter what happened to the prophet. I still believe in prophetic preaching, even to the point of martyrdom, when the bearing of a witness may register so deeply as to move the conscience of a wider community or a later generation. But I now see that truth is not arrived at nor virtue fostered merely by the very satisfying exercise of delivering one's soul. Independent utterance in the pulpit should be free from external restraints, but never from internal restraint. The wise minister will be too humble to assume the role of private prophecy very often or very confidently. I use the term "private prophecy" advisedly. It denotes exactly the difference between the prophetic office of the minister and his function as a citizen. As minister he is the voice of a religious community in which he lives and which in the long run he trusts more than his own private insights. If Christianity has a true social message it is one that a community has validated in its own life. Truly prophetic preaching is preaching that puts into words clearer than the people can command insights deeper than they may have individually attained to, but which are so authentically implicit in their communal experience as Christians that those who hear are con-

strained to say, "Verily, this is the word of God." The
liberty of the pulpit is, I fear, falsely conceived in Protestantism. It is commonly taken as an individual matter—the individual right to prophesy, even when the
preacher is voicing purely private judgments. Such liberty has immeasurable value to the citizen but to conceive prophecy in this individualistic way does violence
to its meaning. True prophecy is representative. As the
priest carries the sins of his people to the altar, so
the prophet voices the moral judgments to which the
people, on their knees before God, feel irresistibly impelled. Let me illustrate this with an incident that made
a deep impression on my own mind.

A minister friend, a noble and courageous soul, told
me that on one occasion some of his laymen criticized
his socially prophetic preaching. He rebuked them,
kindly but plainly with the reply: "Only God goes with
me into the pulpit." He was deeply conscientious; he
believed that by resisting pressure he was doing the
Lord's will. It did not occur to him that he was in effect
arrogating to himself, in violation of the lay principle
on which Protestantism is founded, a peculiar function
in discovering and proclaiming the will of God. He was
giving a new setting to a notorious proclamation:
"Meinselbst und Gott." True, the laymen's criticism
may have been out of place. It may have been an unwarranted attempt to intimidate. But if so it merited a dif-

ferent kind of rebuke—one based on the merits of the case and not on the prophet's immunity from lay criticism.

My point is that on its face any lay criticism of ministerial prophesying is a challenge to the truly representative character of the minister's utterance. It calls, not for defiance, but for a frank and humble effort to show that what the preacher has said is, after all, an authentic expression of the mood of a Christian community as such. Only by carrying conviction that this is true can the Christian minister be more than a free-lance platform speaker. As such he may be a brilliant performer; he may even do much good in his way—but he is not a prophet of the Church. The voice of prophecy is authenticated by its faithful articulation of the mood of a spiritual community.

There is something inevitable about prophecy. All private, fortuitous judgments, all judgments of mere *means* to moral ends, are excluded from prophecy. The authority of love as a way of life that is applicable to all relationships, the sin in exploitation of other human beings, the stewardship of possessions—a much more radical doctrine than socialism, by the way, for it denies private ownership altogether!—these are general truths of Christianity that are inescapable when the Christian tradition is taken seriously. These are things we hold to as corollaries of the centrality of Jesus Christ in the

Christian ethic. We may well define the Christian social message as the faithful and relentless application to every relationship of the truth revealed in Christ. His personality is the complete warrant for the Christian message as an ethical imperative. But practical judgments as to what constitutes at any one time an appropriate embodiment of these absolutes in concrete programs of action—these judgments are qualitatively different. The Church is concerned with them, to be sure, in its educational functions. The minister may deal with them as a part of his educational office. But he cannot say, "Thus saith the Lord, this anti-lynching bill must pass in Congress." He *can* say, "Thus saith the Lord, the voice of thy brother's blood crieth unto me from the ground." Differences there may be concerning social expedients; there can be none about the enormity of the sin.

To interpret this as meaning that the minister should avoid "displeasing" people is, of course, to caricature it, and to miss entirely the meaning of the Church. For the Church is a spiritual community in which people consent to endure the passing of judgment upon their own waywardness and unfaithfulness. Only as its members participate in a vigorous and often painful examination of their own lives can the Church be said to exist at all. An earnest people expects a minister to denounce its sins *but it must be done by appeal to a sanction which they corporately recognize.*

I am quite aware that this sounds simpler than it will be found to be in practice. The Church is often far from "being the Church." Baptism does not overcome stubbornness and much grace is needed to cure the ethical blindness caused by self-interest. Also the very convincingness of a prophetic message may engender rage and bitterness before it brings contrition. It may happen that even the most authentic testimony will be rejected in a given time or place. The prophetic preacher holds his office precariously in times of social stress for he may have to appeal beyond his visible church to the Church that is to be. If he has mistaken his private opinion for the voice of God he will be forgotten. If he is a true prophet his utterances will be vindicated by the larger religious community or in a later day. But the essence of the matter is that the inevitability—the inescapably authentic quality—of a prophetic message is the measure of the prophet's true authority, and of his success. His voice is not his own voice but the voice of the Church.

It is community that incubates life. Herein the meaning of a personalist philosophy becomes explicit. We said that personality can be defined with reference to participation in community experience. This means that the expression of personality is active love. A person, by virtue of being a person, is embarked on a creative enterprise, not just an exploration to find out what kind of universe he lives in, but a demonstration of how much of what love demands can be made actual in the world. I think one of Mr. Niebuhr's paradoxical comments is instructive in this connection. He says that "what religion believes to be true is not wholly true but ought to be true; and may become true if its truth is not doubted." And the scene of man's personal adventure is among the interrelations between persons which constitute society.

But society is huge and complex. Its forms are protean. It does not yield readily to large-scale experimentation. It must be apprehended in microcosm. The Church may be a laboratory of personal living if it is not too large or too diverse. But as we have already noted, it usually is too diverse if not too large. The religious community grows from something small and nascent and vigorous into something large and matured and complacent. "The sect becomes a Church." Thus Christianity began as a small nonconformist compact community, but later became qualitatively almost identical in constituency with the secular community. How shall this contradiction between function and structure be resolved? Manifestly what we have in "sect" and "Church" is not really two alternative kinds of religious organization, but alternating modes of religious community life. The reason why the sectarian group grows outward into the community is not to be found merely in the easy process of secular accommodation. It results inevitably from the universalizing tendency that ethical religion manifests. Redemptive fellowship is irresistibly inclusive. And, conversely, the reason why the Church proliferates into new sectarian groups is that new vision and energy tend to create new structure.

The relevance of the Church to the historical situation in which we live is enhanced by the fact that human brotherhood is our greatest "emergent" in the realm of value. The critical character of the present era is due to the clash between the individual and the personal (social) aspects of life. For the personalist attitude creates the spiritual nexus between individuals which makes the inevitable complexity of modern life endurable. The objective aspect of this increasing complexity we call collectivism. Its spiritual aspect is the personalization of life. Now, the Church in any of its many forms is an instrument by which the culture of personality is maintained on its topmost level. That is to say the Church undertakes to bring all phases of living under spiritual review. It comprehends all the diversities of vocation and explores the *distinctively* human. Even in its sectarian forms the Church has this universal quality. It separates the *accidents* from the *substance* of human life and enthrones something that is common to all men—the quality that we denote by the term *Imago Dei*, the divine image. By discovering this common spiritual nature, and revealing it under the aspect of divine "creation" the Christian community liberates that love which is the active principle of the Christian faith permanently exemplified in the person of Christ. Creative love flowing freely among persons and organizing their common life—this I take to be the meaning of God in history. It is the business of the Church to maintain this creative process which, without institutional provision for its renewal, would be smothered by the material paraphernalia of living. I would go farther and put the matter conversely: whenever this phenomenon of creative fellowship is maintained without reference to ulterior and private purposes there *is* the Church. Barth says the Church is where people listen to God. Quite as true, I think, to say the Church is where people love without restraint.

This conception of the Church is, I believe, fundamental if institutional Christianity is to remain vital in a world that has come to terms with life in a realistic way. For the test of every religious concept, it cannot be too often repeated, is its relevance to what is given in the historical situation. The collectivization of modern life is not, as many political controversialists maintain, a matter of deliberate choice—something to be voted in or out. It is a part of the historically given, the cumulative result, if you will, of a multitude of past decisions, and therefore truly historical, but having the quality of necessity in that no "live" option is presented as to its continuance. To this collectivist trend a meaningful Christianity must be relevant. This is presumably the point of Professor Tillich's impressive comment on group salvation as a religious aim. "While the Christian churches in the Catholic period," he writes, "dealt with the salvation of individuals and with the salvation of groups and institutions only with respect to the church itself, and in Protestantism the salvation of groups and institutions is neglected altogether, the post-Protestant period of Christianity probably will deal predominantly with the ultimate meaning and the salvation of groups and institutions."[2] The Church, conceived as creative fellowship, is a focal point of that transcendence which gives religion its meaning. It is in the world, as religious faith is in man, but not of the world, even as man's faith is not *of* him in an existential sense. Yet the Church's life is continuous with the life of the world in that every aspect of its fellowship projects itself into the life of the community. The carriers of this influence are Christian persons—individuals in whom spiritual community finds expression.

There is in this conception, I think, emancipation

[2] In *The Kingdom of God and History,* Willett, Clark & Company, p. 121.

from the long prevailing confusion over the individual and the social. Again and again we hear it proclaimed that Christianity—and democracy likewise—finds its primary concern in the enriching of the individual person. This is quite true if its meaning is not vitiated by an identification of the two concepts, individual and person. For the two are in an important sense opposed. Properly understood they denote aspects of a bipolar life. A person is of course always an individual, but individuality is a property of anything that has separate existence, whereas personality is a spiritual quality. Personalization is a socializing process, an aspect of community. It proceeds *pari passu* with individuation and therefore is not, like a merely objective and material collectivization, inimical to the individual. The richest experience of community makes the best, the most fully integrated individual. But to order society mainly with reference to the individual, atomistically conceived, is to despiritualize the social process. Democracy is misconceived if it is made to refer all political life to the individual as if the individual, as given, can possibly be an ethical end. When, on the other hand, we find the meaning of democracy in personality we have brought into the picture the ongoing communal life in which the individual finds his meaning. The great bad in totalitarianism is its disregard for personality which is deceptively cloaked in provision for the security of the individual! The individual, so environed, is cut off from the experience of unhampered personal growth. The religious conversion of the individual upon which Christianity has placed so much emphasis consists, then, in incorporation within a spiritual community. It is "entering the Kingdom." The Church is the visible, partial, imperfect society which gives expression to this ideal of a divine community.

The importance of all this for our purpose is that the social message of Christianity for the world as proclaimed by the Church can never be more nor less than the experience—in terms of judgment, aspiration and action—of a worshiping community. When it becomes less than this it is mere "ideology"—an unimplemented idealizing whose purpose is mainly defensive. When it undertakes to be more than this it is "utopian" in an ineffectual and objectionable sense of the word. When regard is had for the communal principle, the slogan "Let the Church be the Church" acquires full validity. There is reason to believe that many who have echoed this cry with enthusiasm have wished it to denote nothing very heroic. To really "be the Church" is to be a fellowship of seeking, of judgment, of decision and of action that go to the very roots of our common life.

I have elsewhere had a good deal to say about an ineffectual social Christianity that expresses itself merely in idealistic pronouncements.[3] I wish here to amplify the judgments thus expressed by saying that official social pronouncements that run beyond any existing practice are valid and useful if they express an authentic corporate conviction rooted in repentance for having "left undone the things we ought to have done." Then they become a true function of the corporate religious consciousness. For corporate worship at its best is an exercise in repentance and aspiration. This is why there is so vital a difference between an affirmation of the Christian mandate of absolute love in the sense of active, creative good will, and a "program" of particulars which is necessarily embedded in relativities and expediencies. It is the business of the Church to pronounce the most thoroughgoing judgments on every aspect of contemporary life, because it is the function of the worshiping community to engender such judgments. With reference to the particular implementation of Christian ideals the Church has a definite responsibility, but it is of a different sort. Here the Church, as a community of Christians, is continually educating its own members in the art of making its spiritual genius operative in every vocational act.

In a word, the Church's moral judgments, flowing as they do from a religious ethic corporately shared, are rendered upon the whole of contemporary life, and

[3] *Church and Society,* The Abingdon Press, Chapter III.

as such are addressed to the world; its activity in the field of implementation, on the other hand, is perforce limited to what its own community can demonstrate in vocational living. If a church body has an authentic corporate conviction that all war is wrong or that all capitalism is wrong it will necessarily embody these absolute convictions in its testimony to the world. But, in the present state of ethical thinking such judgments can, in the nature of the case, flow only from sharply limited sectarian groups, because the Church typically has its roots very deep in the world. By and large, the most that the Church can do in the way of authentic corporate testimony is to affirm the mandate of Christianity that love must be made increasingly operative in the world and to keep insisting on its progressive application in particular situations—always in particular situations. As it develops a religiously motivated discipline within its own membership with reference to particular vocational acts it will effectually and convincingly modify the life of the larger community. For, as Harnack used to say "wherever there is a Church there also is a bit of the world." The life of the Church is continuous with that of the community. Its mission of the "churchification of life," to borrow an expression from the Eastern Orthodox churches, is precisely the extension of its teaching through Christian vocation.

These considerations patently present much difficulty

in the effort to achieve a universal Christian testimony because of the inherent tendency of the Christian community to organize in separate compact bodies whenever its ethical convictions run deep. We have noted that nascent spiritual energy tends to build small disciplined groups, while at the same time Christianity has a universalizing tendency in that it puts the ideal of brotherhood at the center of its ethic. It is a universal personalizing force. Here is an example of the dialectic that characterizes prophetic religion. The disciplined group can express its own ethos only by an expansion that negates its own authority. A process of dilution goes on as the fellowship grows. Without a continually expanding periphery the possibility of embracing the "totally human" is lost. But this very expansion destroys the virility of a small and nascent movement. This phenomenon, as illustrated in the early Church, has been dealt with in two lecture series on the Rauschenbusch Foundation.[4]

The resolution of this conflict can be effected, I think, only by fostering the sectarian type of testimony and practice within the Church so that the heat generated by the small disciplined group shall be liberated inside the Church instead of being forced outside. Vida Scudder, surveying her own spiritual pilgrimage, has

[4] Charles Clayton Morrison, *The Social Gospel and the Christian Cultus*, Series of 1932; and Shirley Jackson Case, *The Social Triumph of the Ancient Church*, Series of 1933, Harper & Brothers.

brought ripe wisdom to bear on this problem. Describing her reflections she says: "Religion is the leaven, not the loaf; and the Church as a whole is loaf, not leaven. But looking back I saw that the minority groups, which represent the leaven, I suppose, were forever the redeeming and truly representative element in that great Body which so often, alas, crucifies the Son of God afresh and puts Him to an open shame. Such minorities have always a prophetic role; and who should say that in critical days like ours they might not play a determining part? With them, I ranged myself."[5] A great insight is here recorded. "The Church is loaf, not leaven." Yet the Church is an authentic community, too, for those who cling to it, even though with scant valor and wavering loyalty, participate in the fellowship of repentance and aspiration. And it is the function of leaven to leaven the loaf by a slow invisible working.

I can hear many of my friends saying, This is surely a low view of the Church itself. The answer is that the Church as part of the world is ever under the judgment of God for participation in the world's sin; but the Church is that part of the world that recognizes the validity of the Christian quest, the part of the community that falls upon its knees. In the act of repentance it has begun to rise above the world!

Curiously enough, the social effectiveness of the

[5] *On Journey*, E. P. Dutton & Co., p. 329.

Church is limited today in part by a spurious application of the principle of independence. The doctrine of the separation of Church and State may actually become anti-social in its implication. Current discussion of the proposal to bring employees of the Church under the coverage of the Social Security Act has made much of the impropriety of subjecting the Church to taxation. This, it is freely alleged, would be a violation of the Church's independence, another encroachment of Caesar. Now, the proposal itself raises many valid issues which are extraneous to the present discussion, but this particular argument is extremely pertinent to the problem of the Church's nature and function. For the Church as a social institution cannot possibly extricate itself from the world. To contemplate any such thing is to misconceive it entirely. Such independence as the Church has does not, in the view here elaborated, rest on an extra-social origin, any more than the "rights of man" rest on any principle that is not socially derived. The State has a duty to facilitate the Church's free functioning because that functioning is one aspect of the social good. In no other sense has the Church any circumscribed domain or any social immunity. A purely formal approach to the question such as many church officials are making may defeat its own ends if carried to its logical conclusion. For if the State has no concern with the Church it certainly should not grant it immunity from taxation—and, incidentally render it more dependent on the State by so doing. But the exemption of the Church from taxation does not rest on any consideration of its *sui generis* character. Rather it results from the application of a broad social principle which puts the Church in the same category with education and philanthropy, which are themselves regarded as secular. No, the Church *as social institution* must discharge full responsibility under principles that are of general application. It must pay its debts, observe the building code and the fire ordinances, and must not disturb the peace—that is, not too noisily! If it has ministers and lay workers whom it supports they are "employees" in the current social meaning of the term and as such have material claims upon their employer of which society must take cognizance. Whether or not they should be brought within the scope of protective legislation is a question to be determined wholly on the basis of social policy in which the Church as an institution has a definite and extensive equity. To claim immunity from common social responsibilities on the ground of spiritual function is to stand the principle of the independence of the Church on its head.

The error underlying the attempt to make the Church stand over against the community and thus to enjoy a special sort of immunity from social controls is a philosophical error. It finds the uniqueness of the Church in its organic, rather than in its functional, character. Organically, it is continuous with the whole community and a part of its normal framework. Functionally, it stands in contrast to all other societies in that it brings them under religious judgment and seeks to influence them by its witness with reference to vocation. The performance of this function requires freedom as does the exercise of any normal function in community life where a pluralistic cultural ideal—as opposed to a totalitarian ideal—prevails. But the Church only makes enemies for itself by claiming a privileged position with respect to social constraints and restraints that are imposed for the general good. This is nothing less than institutional antinomianism, and it is as mischievous as its theological prototype.

The most significant thing that can be said about the Church's social task is that it must be the corporate expression of the spirit of Christ. Its message is a deed more than a word, and that deed is its own incarnation of Christ. The Church has been well called the continuation of the Incarnation. Not that Christ is ever found faithfully expressed in the life of the Church or of its members; no one expects that. But the Church maintains a fellowship consciously oriented toward God, which is the condition of the Real Presence. It is here that the full meaning of a personalist faith appears. The greatest of all miracles is the miracle of personality. The central truth of the Christian faith is embodied in the victorious life of its Founder. For the

Christian community that life is the embodiment of all its beliefs. While much of the current orthodox phraseology seems to be an excessive theological sophistication, it is after all an attempt to express something that is essential to Christian faith. When it is said that the entrance of Christ into the world is a breaking into history of truth that transcends history, the essential meaning, I take it, is that Christ is contemporary to every age. In that sense he transcends history, for he is relevant to every historical situation. The Christian community which is the Church proclaims continually that in Christ love has triumphed over evil, that spiritual death is swallowed up in victory. The Christian social message is the message of redemptive love. The Christian social faith is the faith that redemptive love can be made ever more regnant in the structure of our common life—not only in isolated saintly living, but in the manifold relationships which constitute modern society. Christian discipleship is the determination that the good which can be, shall be. Says Canon Barry: "[The Church's] task is to reconcile to God, through the faith and work of its members, the manifold functions of life in time as the vehicle of the life eternal. It is thus that the true Church comes to be. For this is to fashion in history that Body in which the living Christ is incarnate, and God's reconciling purpose verified."[6]

[6] *Op. cit.*, p. 229.

Chapter V

OUR SECULAR CULTURE

RUNNING through this entire discussion has been a concern that Christian ideals should become inescapably relevant to our common life, to every kind of human relationship. This is what the social gospel means. The "secular" order is to be brought under spiritual sanctions. But liberal Protestantism has, in effect, sustained the secular order against the impact of a long Christian tradition. A curious fact is this preoccupation of liberal Protestantism with what is often called our "anti-Christian social order" while at the same time it has seen little to object to in the secular philosophy that permeates our culture and our educational system. On the one hand, we contend that there can be no boundary between the sacred and the secular. It is this conviction that gives the social gospel its warrant for the application of Christian ethics to the entire structure of society. But, on the other hand, in the name of "the American principle of the separation of Church and State" we effectively maintain the dualism of the sacred and the secular, the spiritual and the temporal.

I am aware that to write in this fashion is to invite rebuke—or contemptuous disregard—on the part of many persons who may up to this point have been reasonably friendly to the position developed. Let me say at once, therefore, that it is no part of the purpose of this discussion to blur the line between Church and State as a boundary between institutional functions. Quite the contrary. The existence of so many church bodies in America, quite apart from any other consideration, makes this distinction between functions imperative. But even if the American people gave allegiance to one religious communion that fact would not remove the distinction between political and ecclesiastical functioning. The Christian ethic involves such a distinction for the reason that the authoritative regulation of human affairs is quite a different thing from the cultivation of the spiritual life by voluntary submission to sanctions maintained by a religious community. This distinction is inherent in the Christian ethic. The Kingdom of God is always a transcendent ideal. Its mandates have a quality of absoluteness, for only the reverent contemplation of a divine society is sufficient to keep men's hearts stoutly devoted to the continual betterment of mankind. We do not rise to our best levels under a command to "be as good as we can" but only under the inexorable command, "Be ye perfect." On the other hand, the maintenance of order and social equilibrium, the restraint of violence and greed involve adjustments and compromises which are the necessary concerns of practical politics. The devising of instrumentalities and procedures by which society, which always gives but partial and intermittent allegiance to spiritual sanctions, may be kept in a tolerable equilibrium is a task for which the Church is not fitted. This is not equivalent to saying, as some theological systems maintain, that the State is evil. That is another affirmation of secularism in a different form. But the State administers, so to speak, the relativities of man's collective life, while the Church exists to bring all relativities under the judgment of a stern and uncompromising ethic.

The difficulty arises, therefore, not with reference to the distinction between Church and State but rather in the inferences commonly drawn from it, particularly in respect to education. It is useless to inveigh against our "anti-Christian civilization" and our "materialistic culture" so long as we educate our children and youth by a system that gives no definitely religious orientation. This issue, I shall try to show farther on, has nothing to do with the exclusion of sectarian teaching from the schools, which the separation of Church and State makes proper and necessary. First, however, it is important that we see the full significance of the secularization of modern life.

[155]

The situation may be thrown into relief by contrasting the modern era with the Middle Ages. We need not draw an idealized picture of medieval Europe in order to see how fundamental a revolution was occasioned by the collapse of the medieval synthesis of spiritual and temporal values. The full import of the fragmentation of the political order that came with the rise of the national States, and of the fragmentation of the spiritual order that resulted from the Protestant Reformation, can scarcely be realized by a modern mind. Dr. Holt in his Rauschenbusch Lectures said:

"The thirteenth century has often been called the greatest century in Western social experience. All social forces seemed at that time to be going in the same direction and there was something of a sense of unity of idea and purpose. The West was an organic society. With the growth of the towns and the development of a trader economy this sense of organic unity gave way to that set of ideas which have been grouped under the general concept of democracy. For the past three hundred years we have been emphasizing the rights and responsibilities of the individual. Men began to explore human society almost entirely from this point of view. They developed certain great slogans—the right of private judgment, the right of free speech, freedom of the press, freedom in education, the right of every religious group to organize as it saw fit, private initiative in business and the right of private property. These principles came to be considered as firmly established; they had been won at great cost and seemed to mark out the pathway of all future progress."[1]

It was the glory of the Middle Ages that men possessed a common faith which had inclusive, universal relevance. No dualism of sacred and secular could be imagined by the medieval mind. The spiritual sanction was invoked when any significant question arose in the ordering of human affairs. A distinguished contemporary Catholic scholar has put the matter in impressive fashion—more impressive because he does not romanticize the Middle Ages. "Some historians," said Etienne Gilson, speaking at the Harvard Tercentenary, "have attempted to describe medieval Europe as endowed with a political unity of its own. It is partly true, and partly an illusion. In a way the Holy Roman Empire always remained a more or less abstract myth; it was a dream that never came fully true, except, perhaps, much later, in the books of its historians. In the same way, it would be just as correct to say that even medieval Christendom never quite succeeded in becoming a concrete and tangible reality. Christendom, that is to say a universal society of all Christians, tied together, even in the temporal order, by the bonds of their common

[1] Arthur E. Holt, *This Nation Under God*, Willett, Clark & Company, p. 66.

faith and common charity; men thinking, feeling, and behaving as true Christians should do, loving and helping each other as true children of the same Father who is in heaven—all those magnificent virtues were perhaps not much more common in medieval societies than they are now. The main difference between our medieval ancestors and ourselves does not lie there, it rather rests with their belief in the absolute value of those virtues. The best among them were fully convinced that there was an order of absolute religious truth, of absolute ethical goodness, of absolute political and social justice, to which differences had to submit and by which they had to be judged. In other words, besides being members of various political and racial groups, those men felt themselves both members of the same Church and fellow citizens in a temporal community whose frontiers were the same as those of Christian faith itself. Irrespective of their various countries, two Christians were always able to meet on the same metaphysical and moral grounds, with the result that no national considerations could ever be allowed to interfere with such questions. Religious life being the same for all, there was no reason why John of Salisbury should not have been appointed as a bishop of Chartres; and why indeed should French people have been appointed as professors at the University of Paris, since better men coming from foreign countries were at hand? They were not asked by the University to teach what was French, but what was true. Thus did it come to pass that, viewing themselves as members of the same spiritual family, using a common language to impart to others the same fundamental truth, those medieval scholars succeeded in living and working together for about three centuries, and so long as they did, there was in the world, together with a vivid feeling for the universal character of truth, some sort at least of Occidental unity."[2]

Now the natural liberal Protestant reaction to this is a shrinking from what at first appears to be its implication of a self-contained, authoritarian system. No Protestant—and certainly not every Catholic—would want to go back to the Middle Ages. Dr. Gilson, himself, warns against any such religious nostalgia. But the important thing that appears in his portrayal is not the ethical absolutism, with its rigid institutional buttressing; rather it is the fact that prior to the modern era men had a common and inclusive frame of reference which made possible in principle what Dr. Holt calls "responsible living" in a world of stark realities.

Professor Reinhold Niebuhr, whose ethical realism guards him from all romanticizing, has made a significant comment on this aspect of the Middle Ages. After

[2] *Medieval Universalism and Its Present Value,* Sheed and Ward, pp. 11-12.

noting the inadequacy of the medieval static conception of society, he adds: "Yet there was in the Middle Ages a religiously inspired sense of social solidarity and mutual responsibility, in comparison with which more than one modern era falls short. To this day the aristocratic sense of *noblesse oblige*, which still lives in some European countries and which is rooted in the spiritual idealism of the medieval period, has excellencies of social attitudes far superior to the ruthless indifference to human needs in the more commercial and industrial classes. The reverence for the value of human personality, the critical attitude toward wealth and luxury, the emphasis upon the love ideal in the Gospel, all these forces of Christianity had a real effect upon the social passion of this period which was so thoroughly dominated by the Christian church."[3]

The philosophic and spiritual significance of the great upheaval that shattered the structure of the medieval world has been strikingly expressed by Will Durant. "Ever since Copernicus," he remarks, "Western man has been struggling to reconceive deity in terms worthy of the universe that Copernicus revealed. It is an epochal task, laid upon man only every two or three thousand years; in the light of its burden we may understand and forgive the disorder of the modern

[3] Reprinted from *The Contribution of Religion to Social Work*, by permission of Columbia University Press, pp. 8-9.

soul. Generations must pass before the transition will be complete, before man will live again, as in the thirteenth century, on some steady level of conduct and belief."[4]

It should be noted that the medieval synthesis of secular and sacred, temporal and spiritual, was nothing novel in idea. What was attempted was the rational organization in society of a principle that was implicit in Hebrew, Greek and Roman thought and life. The Old Testament is impregnated with the concept of theocracy—the rule of God in all the affairs of men. The Greek and Roman pantheons were filled with deities who walked daily upon the earth. Until modern times Church and State were not conceived as distinct in any sense that could make the functions of one irrelevant to the functions of the other.

I have been at pains to emphasize that the thesis here developed is wholly free from any implication that Church and State should not remain separate and have indicated the basic reason for that separation. If I am not mistaken the history of the Middle Ages presents a paradox at this point. Lionel Curtis in his impressive work *World Order (Civitas Dei)* has given a clue to the contradiction. He recognizes the incalculable value of the Church's contribution to the structure of society and sees in Christianity a denial of all dualism between

[4] *Saturday Evening Post,* August 5, 1939.

[161]

sacred and secular. "Yet," he says, "the fullest acknowledgement of its merits cannot alter the fact that Christendom, as organized in the Middle Ages, was, in
principle and therefore in its ultimate effect, the direct
antithesis of the polity which Jesus had conceived as
essential to the ever continuous growth of virtue in
men."[5] Again he says, "The attempt to solve that
problem by creating the Holy Roman Empire as an
instrument for the secular government of the world,
whilst the Church wielded the spiritual power, proved
a disastrous failure, for the basic reason that human
affairs cannot be so divided. In the endless conflicts
between emperors and popes neither Empire nor Pa-
pacy developed the attributes of a genuine government
such as had ruled in the days of the Caesars. Chaos,
maintained in Central Europe and Italy till near the
close of the nineteenth century, was the fruit of those
conflicts."[6]

Here is the paradox: the Middle Ages sought to im-
pregnate all life with a divine ideal and to bring it
under a divine sanction, but by making of the Church
an instrument of power, i.e., a political instrument, it
vitiated its own distinctive efforts. This suggests that
while to isolate any area of life from religious sanction
is a repudiation of Christianity, the Christian ethic

[5] Oxford University Press, page 250.
[6] Page 815.

[162]

cannot become operative in society by the imposition of ecclesiastical control.

Thus secularization in the technical sense of removing ecclesiastical control over the common life must be sharply distinguished from what I have called the secularization of the mind. If Mr. Curtis is right it might have been possible to avoid the ecclesiasticizing of life in the Middle Ages and at the same time to carry much further the spiritualizing influence of the Church upon society.

How great that task would have been, and is today, Canon Lilley has shown in his account of the changes which economic and industrial development produced between the 13th and 15th centuries. Whereas, he says, "in a simpler state of industrial life the Church had been able to assess directly the conditions which governed the application of justice in secular life and to legislate directly about those conditions, she found that, with the growing complexity of the life of secular business, the conditions which determined the application of strict justice became more elusive and obscure. She could indeed, and did consistently, proclaim the traditional principles of Christian ethics in these matters, as, for instance, the condemnation of usury or the definition of the elements which constituted the real value of commodities. But these principles had no longer their old immediacy of application. The yard-measure of the traditional Christian ethic was fast becoming an abstraction for this concrete world where industry depended from day to day upon the possibility of borrowing and where market-price too frequently failed to coincide with even the most liberal interpretation of the just price. In short, industry and commerce, in extending the range and complexity of their operations, had unconsciously developed an autonomy of their own. All that the spiritual authority could do was to accept that autonomy and to humanize or Christianize it in the widest measure of its power."[7]

That Christianity is operative as a "humanizing" agent in the world today none will deny, but the key words in the passage quoted are "to accept that autonomy." The achievement of autonomy by economic and political life is the very substance of secularization as the term is here used. Autonomy for the part means the fragmentation of the whole.

Now it should need no argument to show that this secularization of the modern world is directly related to the disintegration of standards and the collapse of sanctions so widely complained of. To trace these results to a single cause would of course be an oversimplification, but I venture to suggest that the loss of a total spiritual frame of reference by which to evaluate,

[7] A. L. Lilley, in *The Just Price*, Student Christian Movement Press Ltd., pp. 82-83.

to test and to organize human experience is the main cause of the lack of an adequate philosophy of life and the uncertainty, not to say cynicism, with reference to values which conspicuously characterizes our age. The wholesome development of personality requires a high degree of emotional security. This is by no means the same thing as physical security, for nothing is more impressive than the way in which people give themselves to a cause which involves great risk when their souls are stirred by a commanding ideal. Witness the abandon with which the youth of totalitarian countries go to war. Emotional security is attained only when life presents a "total" challenge. The totality may be artificial and the cause tragically deceptive, but where there is a convincing summons to total dedication youth is quick to respond. There is reason to believe that what is happening in Germany today is due primarily to the collapse of a philosophy of life upon which a people had long depended. More will be said on this aspect of the subject in the last chapter, when the fortunes of democracy will be under discussion.

My point here is that what is most conspicuously lacking in contemporary life is a perspective on the whole of life—a *Weltanschauung* which gives the individual a place to stand and enables him to come to terms with his universe. In an insightful little book Professor Edman gives a philosopher's diagnosis of the contemporary spiritual distress. It is not "the setback of principles, of belief in democracy, or in human nature, or in the goods of life, that has been most devastating," he says. "The discovery that principles are wrong, that practices are ineffective, would not trouble us so deeply. What does give us pause is that the instrument on which liberal hopes had above all relied, the instrument of reason itself, has been revealed as so tiny a flicker, so negligible a force, in the governance of mankind. . . .

"We have come, I think, for the first time since the early nineteenth century to the point where, especially among progressive minds, the deep fear has arisen that intelligence itself is pathetically ineffective. For, against all those convenient shibboleths of nineteenth-century hopefulness, comes the stark assertion of force. Fanaticism is in the saddle. Brute power is dominant in civilization, and things have come indeed to such a pass that the very nations which condemn such an assertion of power find that only by brute resistance can brute power itself be repulsed. Good will and good sense indeed! The climax of our disillusion comes in the fact that civilized virtues appear to have no place and no jurisdiction in a world where ill-will and madness prevail."[8]

[8] From Irwin Edman, *Candle in the Dark,* copyright 1939 by Irwin Edman. By permission of The Viking Press, Inc., pp. 35-37.

Thus the fragmentation of the modern world into which the "acids of modernity" have eaten so deeply has inevitably produced bafflement and frustration on the one hand and hardness and cynicism on the other. Religion among us is peripheral to the conduct of affairs. The very ideal of religious freedom to which we do such elaborate homage rests, in too many minds, on a conception of religion as private—mistakenly called "personal"—something to be respected after the fashion of minding our own business. It is commonly appealed to as a negative principle meaning not so much freedom to exercise religion as freedom from being bothered about it.

A discriminating observer has given a pen picture of the secularist trend as seen within a religious organization. Writing about the place of religion in the Young Women's Christian Association, Mary S. Sims says: "There is hesitation, common now over a number of years, about talking of religion and religious subjects, particularly in any personal terms. There is the feeling that such conversation is essentially priggish or unreal, and so we see people go through the cycle from being unwilling to talk about religion because of a sense of unreality to saying that the real element in religion is its social expression in society, and then finally that the social expression in society is the only important element in religion, and at last emphasis on the social

[167]

scene alone with no regard to the spiritual life."[9] This very pat statement is quoted here, of course, solely because it describes not something in any sense peculiar to this one organization, but a very general contemporary mood.

T. S. Eliot has been rather roughly handled by liberal critics for the thesis of his little book, *The Idea of a Christian Society*. It is possible to remain on guard against possible dangerous implications of his argument and yet to see genuine significance in his main contention. Certainly it is a mistake to suppose that it rests on a naïvely romantic conception of human nature which is to be completely regenerated by Christian baptism! "We must abandon," he says, "the notion that the Christian should be content with freedom of cultus, and with suffering no worldly disabilities on account of his faith. However bigoted the announcement may sound, the Christian can be satisfied with nothing less than a Christian organization of society—which is not the same thing as a society consisting exclusively of devout Christians."[10] The last clause is illuminating as to what Mr. Eliot has in mind. Elsewhere he declares that "even if, in the present conditions, *all* persons in positions of the highest authority were devout and orthodox Chris-

[9] "Interpreting the Y.W.C.A. to the Community," *Womans Press,* Vol. XXXI, No. 4, April, 1937, p. 157.

[10] Harcourt, Brace and Company, page 33.

tians, we should not expect to see very much difference in the conduct of affairs."[11] Rather, it is the "general ethos of the people" themselves that determines how society shall be ordered.

No amount of criticism, however well aimed, of the political implications of Mr. Eliot's discussion can lessen the pertinence of his critique of contemporary life. The sanctions which men acknowledge in their individual lives must be made relevant to their corporate behavior, or society must disintegrate.

We are concerned throughout this whole discussion with the development of an adequate social ethic. My contention has been that in our tireless formulation of social creeds and framing of social resolutions we have overlooked the basic problem—the secularization of the modern mind. Before any ethical reconstruction can take place there must be a widespread amenability to spiritual principles that have relevance to the common life. Otherwise religion inevitably becomes escapist. Protestantism has undoubtedly contributed to this result through its emphasis on the autonomy of the individual, and liberal Protestantism has compounded the offense by its nihilistic attitude toward authority. It is very difficult to elicit anything but skepticism for the idea of authority among students who have come up through even our best schools. The idea that there can

[11] Page 25.

[169]

be such a thing as intrinsic authority in the experience of a community without arbitrary imposition by an institution is difficult to win acceptance for. And this, I believe, is due chiefly to the fact that education is typically carried on without specific and continuous reference to the central spiritual values in our culture and without the reverent cultivation of those values which it is the function of religion to maintain. In any case, I shall venture to propose a modification of our educational policy in that direction. I am not prepared to defend it on the basis of experimental evidence because the evidence of history is inconclusive.

It is true that in certain other countries religion has sustained a much closer relation to education than in America and has not produced a golden age. Germany is sure to be cited as an example. In that particular instance I think it is not difficult to show that the influence of Christian ideals upon the common life has been systematically vitiated by the Erastianism (subordination of the Church to the State in the social sphere) which has characterized the Lutheran tradition. A dichotomy between the religious and the secular has been preserved in the German culture, which has been startlingly illustrated by the case of Martin Niemöller, who was willing to fight for the Nazi government so long as it refrained from invading the technical sphere of the Church. In the case of Roman Catholic countries the factor of ecclesiastical domination, as Mr. Curtis has pointed out with reference to the Middle Ages, has probably offset in large part the impact of the Christian ethos upon the common life. England, where the secularism of the prevailing culture inspired Mr. Eliot's essay, has an educational system in which the churches have played a considerable part, but it seems quite accurate to characterize that system as secular in spirit. Commenting recently on the educational situation the London *Times* said: "In every other subject the educational authority rightly demands a high standard of competence from its teachers. But if those who give religious instruction have had no training for the work, or if a head teacher is openly antagonistic to Christianity, the state regards such matters as outside its purview, and does not interfere. While it maintains that the teaching of religion should be left mainly to the churches, it will only admit representatives of the churches exceptionally and under severe restrictions to teach religion in its schools. Again and again the odious fallacy recurs that education is one thing and religious instruction quite another."[12] This indicates that the British situation is not unlike the American with reference to the matter under discussion.

Without further speculation concerning the cultural situation in other countries let us consider the issue on

[12] February 17, 1940.

[171]

its merits with reference to our own country. I wish to discuss it under three heads: (1) factors in the secularization of education; (2) the implications of secularization for educational philosophy; (3) an approach to a solution of the problem.

(1) Factors in the secularization of education in America.

Broadly speaking it may be said that education in this country came to be a function of the State—or, more accurately, of the whole community—because of the existence of religious sectarianism on a large scale. (The word "sectarianism" is used here in its common signification and has no relation to the technical distinction between "sect" and "church" which was referred to in the preceding chapter.) This condition operated in two ways. First, it created a situation in which entrusting education to the churches, in accord with the earlier tradition in Europe and in the Colonies, would have given rise to a number of small competing educational systems, inadequate and inefficient. Secondly, it confronted educators with the prospect of continuous sectarian strife within the schools if religion, in a form unacceptable to particular religious groups in the community, should be taught.

That education developed in modern Europe as a function of the Church, largely under the stimulus of the Reformation, is well known. The religious aims of education in the Colonies may be appreciated best by a perusal of early classics such as the New England Primer. This famous schoolbook appeared about 1690 and was in circulation as late as the middle of the last century. It contained an alphabet of lessons composed of verses from the Bible, the Lord's Prayer, the Apostles' Creed and the Westminster Shorter Catechism. Dr. Reisner records that "in some editions appeared John Cotton's 'Spiritual Milk for Babes Drawn out of the Breasts of Both Testaments.' Another frequently appearing item was: 'A Dialogue between Christ, Youth, and the Devil.'" He points out that the primer was religious "in the strict and narrow sense of Calvinistic orthodoxy. With its passing an intellectual and social era had come to an end."[13]

Cubberley says of education in the Colonial period: "The most prominent characteristic of all the early colonial schooling was the predominance of the religious purpose in instruction. One learned to read chiefly to be able to read the Catechism and the Bible, and to know the will of the Heavenly Father. There was scarcely any other purpose in the maintenance of elementary schools."[14] And Nettels in a recent able work on American history remarks: "Foremost among

[13] Edward H. Reisner, *The Evolution of the Common School,* Macmillan Company, pp. 48-49.

[14] Ellwood P. Cubberley, *Public Education in the United States,* Houghton Mifflin Co., p. 41.

the cultural influences inherited from Europe was the religious impulse. The medieval union of education and religion had not been dissolved when the colonies were founded. To the colonial clergy more than to any other group belonged the task of preserving and fostering learning in the New World."[15]

Students of education always find amusement in the quaint wording of the celebrated Law of 1647 in Massachusetts, a measure of the utmost historical importance, the preamble of which solemnly records that it had been "one chief point of that old deluder, Satan, to keep men from a knowledge of the Scriptures."

This preoccupation of education with religion was possible in communities that were religiously homogeneous, since such a community had nothing to fear from its schools on this score. But as the community became more and more differentiated religiously, difficulty inevitably arose. Horace Mann's crusade for truly public schools in Massachusetts in the 1830's and '40's was an epic struggle, motivated by no antireligious feeling or intent, but rendered inevitable because of the religious situation.

A significant feature of the public-school movement was the alignment of the Protestant churches with it in conscious opposition to Catholic pressure. Catholic

[15] Curtis P. Nettles, *The Roots of American Civilization*, F. S. Crofts & Co., p. 485.

[174]

theory, as every one knows, rests education upon religion, and hence makes it a function of the Church.
Catholics, therefore, living in a non-Catholic country
are compelled by their philosophy to maintain a school
system of their own. The compulsion of their faith,
combined with a sense of the unfairness of "double taxation" for the support of schools, led them to seek sub-
sidies from public funds in order to equalize the burden
as between themselves and non-Catholic citizens. This
policy brought upon them criticism from Protestants
who interpreted it as hostile to the public schools and
as an attack upon the principle of the separation of
Church and State. Although in spirit unfair, this interpretation was essentially true, for Catholic theory
necessarily opposes secularism in education and Catholic political philosophy affords no basis for a secular
state. The latter position, it may be noted, puts American Catholics in an awkward position, since the roots
of the Catholic philosophy with reference to the State
are in the Middle Ages and no authoritative body of
doctrine has been formulated with reference to a non-
Catholic State. Hence American Catholics are in the
position of trying to accommodate themselves to a
political situation which their historic philosophy con-
demns. This position merits sympathetic understanding.

The Protestant attitude for a century has been dictated, I think it may be said, by strategy rather than

philosophical judgment. For underlying the Protestant position has been the rather naïve assumption that if the public schools could be protected from Catholic encroachment through drawing off funds for parochial schools or influencing school policies in other ways, the religious interests of the community would be well served. Until recently there has been little serious consideration in Protestant circles of the effects of secularism in education on religious attitude and outlook.

In part the Protestant attitude toward the exclusion of religion from the schools was no doubt determined by the rise of the Sunday-school movement, which many believed would compensate any loss in religious influence occasioned by a secularist policy. The reception of this new movement, which was becoming strong at the very time when the present public-school policy was in the making, was quite romantic. Vastly more was expected of the Sunday schools than they ever could achieve. Recognition of this attitude, however, helps to explain the general acceptance of what in the light of Colonial history is seen to have been a revolutionary change in education.

It is probably true that the mood of the political founders of this country was influential in giving education a secular orientation. The intellectual leaders among them had religious convictions—no doubt about that—but they were rather in the deistic than the orthodox Protestant tradition. This gave them a rather antiecclesiastical slant and must have made them less than enthusiastic about religious education as commonly conceived. We cannot credit Thomas Jefferson with exerting great political influence and ignore the effect of his deistic religious outlook on the public mind. Furthermore, the population was mostly outside the churches, which suggests that the dominant religious emphasis in Colonial education may have been due more to the influence of the clergy and their following among the intellectuals than to any widespread religious concern. If this is correct, it seems probable that the population as a whole was more sympathetic with the political arguments for general education—the need of a literate and informed electorate—than with traditional religious arguments.

It seems clear, however, that whatever factors entered into the secularization of American education, the intent was never to do violence to the place of religion in the cultural tradition. This is the essential point to keep in mind if one would have a true historical perspective on the present situation.

(2) The implications of secularization for educational philosophy.

Reference was made above to the assumption that the advent of the Sunday school would offset the lack of religious education in the public schools. The fallacy in that assumption is in part recognized today, but only in part. The limitation of time and the inadequacy of the teaching staff would in themselves render the Sunday schools powerless to do more than mitigate the effect of the secularization of the public schools. These weaknesses have led to the development of week-day religious education under church auspices, a movement which in some localities has greatly extended the teaching activities of the churches.

But the major problem remains untouched for it concerns the nature and function of the entire educative process. More and more educators are coming to regard education as a unitary process which concerns the total experience of a growing person. It does not admit of fragmentizing without violence to its essential character. This does not mean, of course, that any particular phase of education as carried on in school cannot be effectively supplemented by an extra-school agency. But it does mean that any phase of education which has no recognition in the public-school program is likely to be a marginal interest on the part of the pupil. This is not serious in the case of special interests which become organized in out-of-school activities, but it is of the essence of religion that it should inform the whole of life. If not central in thought and life it becomes impotent. The institution which has chief responsibility for fixing the general pattern of life in the growing child is almost certain to be the chief contributor to the formation of religious attitudes. That these attitudes turn out to be largely negative is what makes the matter serious.

Confusion readily arises here with reference to the function of the home. It is true that in theory—both Catholic and Protestant—the home is the primary factor in religious education. But this means, in effect, only that a religious home is likely to rear religiously minded children. Undoubtedly where the home is a strongly positive religious influence it tends to be the dominant force in that respect. But we may say the same thing about other kinds of influence. One might even contend that if homes were all they should be the responsibility of the schools for character building would be much less. The public school does not exist for a function that can be neatly defined in relation to that of other agencies, but rather as the instrumentality for inducting the young into the culture at its best. It is the function of the school to rise above the cultural level of the home *as is*. The school is a selective instrumentality with reference to the culture. We expect it to lift the level of the common life. The average American home is no more in position to carry responsibility for the religious education of children and youth than it is to conduct their political education. The home contributes on its own level to every phase of education, but the school must carry the major responsibility for the educative process as a whole. This means that every phase of wholesome education must have its place in an integrated system.

To contend that the Church has shirked its educational responsibility is beside the point. Its responsibility in a society which carries on general education under community auspices is quite different from that of the school, which in the nature of the case is building a total outlook on life and guiding the child in organizing its values. The proper educational function of the Church on the elementary and secondary levels is to induct children and youth into a religious fellowship. It has its own philosophy, its own liturgy, its own peculiar organization of religious life, and its own program of missionary activities. All these functions require for their efficient conduct a basic orientation toward religion which general education should furnish. To hold the Church responsible for the development of a religious outlook is to expect something to be achieved against an adverse influence emanating from a secularized education.

Consider for a moment the net result in terms of religious attitude of the current trend in education to build the curriculum on life experiences. This is an excellent principle, which looks in the direction of the integration of the culture. Whatever is significant in the life of the community is supposed to find its way into the school. Through the social studies the school has become in an impressive way continuous with the life of the community, as it should be. But this process stops abruptly at the door of the church, because of the taboo against introducing religion into public education. This is not because school teachers and administrators are hostile to religion. For the most part it is safe to say they are sympathetic with the aims of the churches and they participate in enormous numbers in church activities. The situation is dominated by fear —fear of arousing prejudices and fear of "starting something" that will destroy the independence of the schools.

A basic difficulty is the false assumption as to what "teaching religion" is. It is a curious anomaly that many educators who have adopted a modern philosophy of education, and who conceive it in terms of free inquiry, still assume that religion can be taught only as sectarian indoctrination. They are convinced that civics can be taught without an effort to standardize political ideas, that economics can be taught without propagandizing for particular theories, but they see in religious education only the inculcation of a particular faith. And in this curious inconsistency they are supported by many religious liberals. It may be granted at once that the introduction of religion into the school program does imply a religious assumption on the part of the education system. That assumption is that participation in religious worship and religious activity is a normal phase of life in a community. It has no more to do with sectarian commitments than the assumption underlying political education has to do with the relative merits of parties. But this basic assumption, I contend, is justified and even obligatory in a democratic nation in which religion has a recognized place in the culture. The exclusion of religion from the schools is a policy which would be wholly consistent in a nation committed to an antireligious philosophy. This is the case in some countries, but not in America.

As for the contention that "religious liberty" requires a rigid exclusion of religion from the schools, I think this familiar slogan will bear a good deal of reexamination. As used in the early Colonial period it meant quite clearly liberty for a community to worship as the consciences of its members dictated. It did not mean simply individual freedom. It was the expression of group purpose, of community need. It is often pointed out that this ideal of religious liberty degenerated into intolerance toward all dissenters. This is true, and it was a fault in the religious outlook of the Puritans that they were so ready to standardize religious experience. But it is important to note the reason for this tendency. Underlying the demand for religious liberty was the conviction that worship was an indispensable phase of wholesome community life. This end could not be attained merely by the proclamation of religious freedom as an individual matter. The current appeal to this principle in support of a secular way of life that relegates religion to the realm of the purely private totally distorts the meaning of religious liberty as a cultural ideal. Its effect is to divorce religion from the major activities of the community. Increasingly the principle of religious liberty is now being seen as a positive principle expressing the need for religious expression as a part of the corporate life of a people. In other words, it means freedom to participate in religious worship and activity—not simply freedom to avoid it. And such freedom can be realized only when the education of the young makes them intelligent about religion and predisposes them toward a positive appraisal of its resources. This, it will be said, is a value judgment. Precisely so, but it is a judgment, I believe, which the American people as a whole support. Their religious concern is now thwarted by fear and the weight of precedent.

The problem, then, becomes one of incorporating the common religious aspirations of a people in their common life without doing violence to any individual conscience. This last is of vital importance. It is not to be provided for, however, by the simple expedient of letting the dissenters decide what the community as a whole shall do. We do not follow that course with reference to any other basic cultural interest. We find ourselves today in the anomalous position of trying to invoke, as a resource for the nation in a time of crisis, religious sanctions which we have deliberately relegated in our educational system.

The liberty of the individual child or youth to abstain from any activity or observance against which he or his parents may have conscientious scruples should be fully guarded. I would not constrain even an objector against saluting the flag when the objection is based on conscientious belief. Here is an area in which we may well lean far backward rather than defy conviction, however fanciful. But when the community as a whole has made up its mind as to the recognition that should be given in its schools to religion as a phase of the culture the liberty of dissent can be, and should be, accorded on an individual basis, without nullifying a general policy.

It must not be supposed that this issue is one of Church and State. The Church has no business to dictate what shall be taught. Personally, I regard current efforts to introduce sectarian instruction into the schools by bringing in priests, rabbis and ministers to teach the children of their respective faiths as an intrusion by the Church. If a community desires it and the courts uphold it, perhaps the paramount importance of local democratic control in education justifies concurrence, but I am convinced it is the wrong way. It is a confusion of institutional functions. Sectarian instruction is precisely what has been excluded from the schools by law. It is of the utmost importance that the distinction between "sectarian" and "religious" be not blurred by such practices as I have referred to. By virtue of the almost complete uniformity of usage in state laws and constitutions, sectarian rather than religious teaching has been banned. There can be no shadow of doubt as to the intention to exclude the former. I hope that we shall not prejudice the situation with reference to the relation of religion to public education by an injudicious breaking down of the principle of the separation of Church and State in America. The giving of sectarian instruction is no business of the schools. Nor is it their responsibility to act as truant officer in requiring attendance at classes conducted outside the schools. I would even say that the giving of credit for any instruction that is not supervised by the school itself is a very questionable practice and is, in effect, a blurring of the boundary line between Church and State. And such supervision is out of place where sectarian teaching is involved.

The contention, however, that religious teaching is necessarily sectarian is without foundation. The word "sectarian" does not define a fixed category of beliefs. For purposes of law and administration it can only be a factual category, having reference to the effect of a given kind of instruction on the community as a whole. That which tends to divide the community is *de facto* sectarian. What other way is there to define it?

(3) An approach to a solution of the problem.

If it be granted that a new definition of policy is needed, it is important that practical procedures be worked out that will admit of experimentation and revision. There is danger at the moment that policies may be adopted in communities here and there without due regard to what is involved.

To begin with, there must be an interfaith approach in the local community to the consideration of the whole question. I said earlier that it is not the business of the Church to make school policy. On the other hand it is a responsibility of the community to require of the schools the kind of product that it expects and the Church functions here as a part of the community. Educational policy is a matter for the people as a whole to determine. In a religiously heterogeneous community citizens of different faiths must agree on the objectives of education, and the religious leaders have a right and a duty to appraise the consequences of present educational policies in religious terms. It is not their sole responsibility, but the initiative is theirs.

This is inherent in the concept of a functionally organized society.

Furthermore, since the secularization of education has come about because of the existence of religious groups that are often antagonistic to each other, there must be a sort of interfaith front—not to "gang up" on the schools, but to take responsibility for removing the chief obstacle to a frank acceptance by the schools of their responsibility for making the educational program consistent with the place of religion in the culture. When the various faiths can say to the educators, "There is no longer any obstacle to your giving religion the same recognition that other phases of our common culture receive," they will have put the responsibility of devising educational procedures on the school where it belongs.

The place to begin in effecting this reorientation is, I think, in the social studies program. The assumption earlier referred to, that participation in religious worship and religious activity is a part of normal adult behavior, dictates that the same frank approach be made to a study of the churches as is now made to the study of the industries, the press, the government and the cultural activities of "our town." Where are the churches? *What* are the churches? Why do people go to them? What are their common interests and what are their main differences? What activities do they

[187]

carry on? This, it may be said, is studying *about* religion, not studying religion. Quite so. Studying *about* is the beginning of *study*. It is the way an orientation is effected. But such inquiry has in it the element of participation based on interest. It is in the nature of group exploration—an "activity program." It is co-operative in a very explicit way, for there will always be members of the various churches in the student group who can give their fellow students the benefit of their own knowledge. (Incidentally, this might prove an excellent exercise in tolerance and mutual appreciation.)

The educational purpose in all this would be not to accumulate information but to domesticate religious interest, so to speak, in the school environment. This sensitization to religious concern as something belonging to the common life is all important. The project of exploration might well go as far as the active interest of the students will carry it. There will doubtless be interviews with church leaders and parish visitors and with church organists and others who can answer questions. The result to be hoped for is the formation of a habit of looking for the religious aspects and implications of all social studies—history, economics and the rest. In a word, what I am after is the progressive de-secularizing of the mind.

As for specifically religious subject matter, an amazing amount of it would be uncovered in the exploration just sketched and the trail will lead into all the disciplines included in the curriculum. The Bible would be studied as the major religious classic of America— particularly the Old Testament, as a common inheritance of Christian and Jew. This suggestion is often met with the question, "Do you mean just *as literature*?" To which the reply must be, "Of course, but as religious literature, for that is what it is." The Bible should be studied in the schools for the same purpose for which it is studied in the churches—except as the latter may involve specific doctrinal interpretations authoritatively presented. It should be studied as a spiritual resource, a deep well from which men have drunk through the centuries.

This approach to religion in the schools would, of course, involve the preparation of teachers. The teacher-education institutions will not be slow to respond to a call from the field. I have known scores—hundreds, I think—of teachers in training who would have been glad to add to their preparation the ability to teach religious classics on their particular professional level. And what is even more important, they would welcome expert help in the training institution in understanding the religious factors in history and biography and the religious aspects of philosophy and political science. What is needed above all else is the opening of minds, in teachers and students, to the resources of religion.

Along with intellectual inquiry goes the cultivation of an attitude of reverence. I believe that our teachers of art and dramatics should be encouraged to recover the religious motive which has been so influential in their fields of interest and make it articulate. I believe that simple forms of group worship will be developed naturally in the life of the school once a new orientation is effected and suspicion and fear have broken down. There has been ample demonstration of the possibility of interfaith worship of the most rewarding kind.

Again and again as I have been writing this it has come to my mind that everything I have mentioned is probably being done somewhere! This is one of the difficulties of the situation. No one knows to what extent the pressure of spontaneous community interest in religion has already broken through tradition. I hope this need for information will soon be supplied. For we are in the position of being dominated by a tradition whose strength is in habit more than in reason. We need co-operative experimentation with co-operative evaluation of results.

I have devoted so much space to this subject, which is rarely treated in a book on Christian ethics, because of my conviction that the main obstacle in American life to the growth of an effective social ethic is the disease which I have called the secularization of the mind. If that fault is to be remedied our common religious heritage must be recovered in our educational system.

Chapter VI

CHRISTIANITY AND WAR

WHEN these lectures were given the European War was still only a menacing cloud on the horizon. By the time they appear in print it may have resulted in a quick victory for the Axis Powers or settled into a test of endurance. Already its cost in human life has been staggering. I propose to write nothing in this chapter that will be affected one way or the other by American involvement in the war, should that come to pass. At this writing the outlook for Europe is dark indeed, and the possibility that this country may be drawn in is now being soberly reckoned with by people who scoffed at it but a few weeks ago. Should the possibility become actuality the situation of the American churches will be just what it is today for their sister churches in belligerent nations. Indeed, if the ecumenical principle means anything the Church is now involved, for the *Una Sancta* has been violated. Our Christian brothers are fighting now, or refusing to fight if their consciences restrain them, and the Church universal is not above the battle but in it.

The war has confronted the Christian churches with the necessity of taking stock of those resources of peace which they had assumed were being built up in such degree as to make so savage an outbreak of human passions only a remote possibility. They are also having to re-examine their own testimony on war and peace. For two decades the Protestant churches have been vigorously denouncing war. It has been characterized as the devil's business, "the world's chief collective sin," "nothing that Jesus meant and everything that he did not mean." Church assemblies have highly resolved not to "bless war" again. Much honest contrition has been manifested by Christian ministers who were convinced that in the last war they had failed Christ by not standing resolutely against the whole "bloody business."

And now the war has come, and if we in America are immune from its ravages most of us are under no illusions as to the reason why. Nations do not fight merely for sentiment, though soldiers often do. Nations do not fight except when corporately convinced that their "vital interests" are at stake. And when they are so convinced they usually fight. This is simple realism about governments and peoples. It is an old pattern that seems to be as rigidly held to as ever in the past. I am not suggesting that it should be so or that it always will be so, but only that it is so. War reveals the deep cleft between politics and idealistic ethics. It is only one of the evidences of that cleavage, but it is the most vivid and terrible example of it.

It follows from the very nature of an ecumenical Christianity that if there is a Christian testimony concerning war it must be a universal testimony. There can be no geographical limitation of that testimony. If American Christians invoke the sanction of their faith against participation in the war as necessarily wrong they can do so only as convinced pacifists who believe that British and French and Canadian Christians would have done better to take the same course. In other words, if the judgment against participation by Christians applies to this country only it is a relative judgment, a judgment rendered in the field of practical ethics, rather than a universal testimony against war as wrong per se. Such practical judgments have to be made, but only confusion and gross unfairness to fellow Christians in the battle zones can result from the effort to invoke a general sanction for a course that has been possible for us in America only because of the Atlantic Ocean. For the convinced pacifist the universalizing of Christian testimony on war is possible and altogether logical, but for non-pacifist Christians the necessity remains of formulating a truly ecumenical judgment that will be as applicable to European Christians as to Americans. The American churches cannot say that conscientious Christians in Europe may fight and still be Christians if they insist on determining their own course by reference to an absolute sanction against war.

Now, I believe it is precisely because the peace movement among the American churches has lacked this discrimination between absolute and relative ethical judgments that we are in such confusion at the present time. The method followed has been to get church bodies and assemblies committed against war in general and to pledge ministers and lay Christians to war resistance as the only course consistent with the anti-war testimony of ecclesiastical bodies. It must be recognized that this movement has had a profound and authentic moral quality. The convinced pacifist is in duty bound to make converts, and it is the most natural thing in the world for one so convinced to put all war in one category and condemn it unconditionally. But what has happened in America is that voluminous church resolutions have been passed in which war was condemned in this fashion without any real analysis of the ethical situation confronted. This has involved our churches in grievous inconsistencies and contradictions. Leaders of the peace movement who were pacifists themselves have with reason exclaimed, "If war is the heinous thing you say it is, how can any Christian possibly participate in it?"

The trouble, I think, is that the framers of our antiwar resolutions, under the stress of strong moral feeling, have allowed themselves to make of war an undifferentiated concept which lumped together all kinds of *warfare*, while the majority of those who voted for these resolutions never regarded them as condemning participation in war *no matter how the particular war might be precipitated*. What I am saying here is not a matter of opinion; it is a matter of record.

The Methodist Church—to cite the largest Protestant body and one in which antiwar sentiment has been very pronounced—at the Uniting Conference in April, 1939, declared: "We believe that war is utterly destructive and is our greatest collective social sin and a denial of the ideals of Christ. We stand upon this ground, that the Methodist Church as an institution cannot endorse war nor support or participate in it." The Conference also put the authority of the Church behind the refusal of military service on grounds of conscience.

The General Assembly of the Presbyterian Church, U. S. A., declared in 1938: "War is a denial of faith in the God of love and justice." It also upheld the right of Presbyterian students to refuse military training.

Yet both these bodies, which may perhaps be taken as fairly typical, made clear that they were not pronouncing participation in war unconditionally wrong.

[196]

The statement of the Methodist General Conference above referred to, giving support to conscientious objectors, is followed immediately by the declaration, "We recognize the right of the individual to answer the call of his government in an emergency according to the dictates of his Christian conscience." And the action of the Presbyterian General Assembly referred to above contains these words: "There are those who believe that peace can only be assured by a policy of complete isolation through neutrality and those who believe that peace can only be assured by complete participation in international action designed to enforce peace through economic and other pressure. Between these two groups are to be found all intermediate gradations of opinion, conscientiously held by Christian people."

By far the most representative recent pronouncement by a non-Roman Christian body is that of the Oxford Conference of 1937. The report on "The Church and War" included these strong words: "War involves compulsory enmity, diabolical outrage against human personality, and a wanton distortion of the truth. War is a particular demonstration of the power of sin in this world and a defiance of the righteousness of God as revealed in Jesus Christ and Him crucified." At the same time it summarized three quite different positions which are held by conscientious

[197]

Christians, ranging from refusal of participation to the belief that "normally a Christian should take up arms for his country."

That such wholesale denunciations of war in general are in some sense inconsistent with the dispensations given to individuals who might conscientiously engage in war must be freely granted. Yet the explanation is not far to seek. There is a sense in which war may be unconditionally denounced under a Christian sanction without raising the pacifist issue. The formula for it was actually furnished in a secular document—the Kellogg-Briand Pact. What was denounced therein was the resort to war "as an instrument of national policy." The congressional debates made it abundantly clear that the question of defensive war was not involved. If there was a fatal weakness in that document it was not in the content of it but in the assumption on the part of the signatories that in the existing state of the world *all* the ratifying powers would impose upon themselves the restraints necessary to give it effect. Likewise, underlying the antiwar resolutions of the churches was the same reservation—but it was not made explicit. There was no assumption of responsibility for the consequences when some nation in defiance of Christian teaching should actually precipitate war. This should certainly have been made clearer. It is muddy thinking to lump into one category a variety of forms of behavior and pronounce an indiscriminate judgment upon them. But this is a fault common to all our moralizing. We deal too much in *nouns* and not enough in *verbs*. That is to say, we approach issues conceptually instead of *operationally*, and thus obscure fine ethical distinctions—which later, when confronted with an actual situation, we insist on making. Perhaps this is the only way large bodies can make moral progress. They see things first under an aspect of universality and formulate general rules which in the light of experience have to be broken down into particulars. This is the task we must face now that the Church as an ecumenical institution confronts war in the concrete. It is no easy task, and it has its dangers.

First among these dangers, perhaps, is that of a wholesale denunciation of the pacifist philosophy. Already there are abundant signs of a revulsion from that way of thinking which for some years after the World War had so prominent a place in the pulpit and in the religious press. Pacifism must be appraised not as a proposed national policy, but as an individual way of life. To be sure, any serious movement may claim the right to make its own definitions, but it is to be feared that much of the current discussion of pacifism suffers from want of clarity as to what pacifism means. Only when it presents itself as a mode of resistance to participation in war, on the part of individuals and minority groups, does it raise an ethical issue within the Christian community. For pacifism never becomes an issue of national policy on the ethical plane. The pacifist is under no obligation to prove that his "way" would be practicable in a given situation—any more than an ethical socialist who eschews private possessions is under obligation to establish the practicability of his course as a universal pattern in the existing state of society. One of the best statements of the pacifist position I have ever read is contained in an article by Winnifred Wygal, from which the following passage is taken: "Pacifism is a level of being religious which far outstrips the achievement of the average Christian. There are but few pacifists in the world in any period in history and they are moral giants. Such pacifism is a religious vocation in the Catholic sense of the word vocation. Not every Catholic enters a monastery and not every sincere Christian is a pacifist but the analogy is not farfetched. In this sense pacifism is not a theory or an external method; it is a way of life. It determines and is determined by everything that the individual is and does.

"Although Gandhi is not a Christian, his pacifism is of this variety. It is rooted in the Ultimate and the Unconditioned. Men like Canon Raven, Richard Gregg and George Lansbury are pacifists in the sense of a kind of saint-hood, of being called to a vocation of almost mysterious quality. The early history of the F.O.R. in the United States illustrates this spirit. It is a story of moral courage and clarity born of prayer and genuine sacrifice in which a few people stood alone and in danger for the truth of God as they saw it. This is not the moment to say, as countless people today do, 'Such men only confuse the issue.' They confuse the issue no more and no less than any person who has a profound conviction and acts upon it confuses the issue for men who do not share his experience. St. Francis of Assisi greatly confused the issue for the Pope. The conviction that one group of men confuse the issues of history more than another group depends upon one's perspective. It is necessary, in any case, to accept the objective fact that there is a small group of people in the world for whom the religious vocation means pacifism pure and absolute and primary. The moral stature of individuals to whom pacifism means something as fundamental as this is indisputable."[1]

Every person who has a well-functioning conscience recognizes some limits of ethical accommodation beyond which he will not go. He will sacrifice possessions, profession, home and even reputation rather than do what would violate irremediably his sense of honor.

[1] "Pacifism as a Religious Vocation," in *Radical Religion*, Spring, 1939, Vol. IV, No. 2, p. 37.

The pacifist recognizes such a moral boundary at participation in war. Being what he is, he must refuse. The authentic quality of this position is recognized in the religious demand that governments respect conscientious objection to military service. It is one of the few bright spots in the present world situation that this principle should have won so large a measure of observance. But this is a moral height that is precariously held. There must be resolute defense of that position. The coercion of conscience is in itself an impairment of national integrity; respect for conscience is in itself an instrument of national defense. If conscientious objectors should become so numerous as to impair national defense it would be evidence that the world is much nearer to learning the lesson of peace.

But, having said this, I am constrained to add that many pacifists have a way of transforming their faith from a personal spiritual conviction into a political strategy. When a pacifist member of a church assembly contends sharply for collective commitments that only persons who share his absolutist convictions can consistently make, he ceases to be a good moralist and becomes a poor politician. The politics of peace cannot, in the nature of the case, be pacifist—except for a nation of pacifists, and there is no such thing. A pacifist bearing his nonconformist testimony is a splendid spectacle, but a pacifist struggling to wrest extreme commitments from a deliberative assembly made up of people who do not share his convictions is something less. The article quoted above contains another impressive passage which I cannot forbear to reproduce here: "Pacifism which is a religious vocation is asceticism and cannot in the nature of the case function politically. There is a distinction between a Lansbury who resigns from the House of Commons because the British government does not and cannot scrap its empire in the interest of a warless world and those so-called pacifists who seek to influence the government to act as the Christian pacifist would act, which is the distinction between a saint who accepts the limitations of his position for practical politics and the man whose position becomes a contradiction in terms, because he seeks at one and the same time to be an individual absolutist and a political lobbyist. Here it is that the religious pacifist, called to a life of redemptive love, must see that he is politically inept and find his function elsewhere than in that aspect of the historical process which is engaged in contemporary political strategy."[2]

The most grievous aspect of war from the Christian point of view is of course the hate that it engenders. A news service from France that lies on my desk con-

[2] *Ibid.*, pp. 38-39.

tains the following biting words from the letter of a French soldier: "My grandfather fought the Germans in 1870, and in 1870 the Germans were not Nazis. My father fought the Germans in 1914, and in 1914 Hitler was nothing. Now, I fight the Germans and I don't care a damn whether they are Nazis or not. The only thing that I want is that my son (age 10 months) should not be compelled to run under machine-gun fire in 25 years' time through the fault of idiotic statesmen who dream that Germany can be made bigger and better. We French soldiers—all my comrades think the same—are not fighting for Justice and Right, or to make the world safe for *Democracy. We fight to destroy Germany. . . .*" Comment is unnecessary.

Over against that I would put the following from the pen of an English churchman in the early weeks of the war: "It does not seem possible that in the long run Hitler could win a military victory over us, but there is always the peril that he might win a spiritual victory. If by this war which he has thrust upon us he should induce in us bitterness or callousness or vengefulness or brutality or a narrow selfishness of national life, to that extent he will have defeated us, and the war will have been in vain."[3] What is happening, of course, and what always happens in war,

[3] "Ilico" (Dr. Nathaniel Micklem) in the *British Weekly,* September 21, 1939.

is that the fine sensitiveness revealed in the second quotation degenerates and is replaced by the brutal hardness of the first. This is the spiritual tragedy of war.

The fact remains, however, that it is the predominant testimony of the Christian community that this tragedy is inherent in life as it has to be lived in the world today. I believe we should be farther on our way to a Christian testimony concerning war if much of the zeal that has gone into securing passage of out-and-out antiwar resolutions in church assemblies had been put into patient analysis of the issue and a more dispassionate formulation of ethical judgments. The evil of which I am now speaking is evident in its fruits. The habit of condemning war as if it were one un-differentiated kind of behavior has wrought havoc with many sensitive souls who when confronted by a situation in which they saw no moral alternative to participation in armed conflict were left entirely without any religious sanction for their conduct. The logic of the situation seemed to be clear: War is essentially unchristian. Hence, if a Christian fights he forsakes the faith. But my duty as a citizen requires that I should fight. Hence I have no alternative but to abdicate as a Christian in order to do my duty as a citizen. This dilemma is brought closer by a realistic theology which recognizes that even the Church "has its roots in a sinful world," and that perfection is not attained in this life. If, however, war is recognized as the devil's business, when one engages in it, he must fly the devil's flag. So runs the argument.

The situation thus created has in it the elements of moral tragedy: one is confronted by a necessary choice between two courses both of which appear morally wrong. The most striking and recent illustration of it that has come to my attention occurred not in the Christian but in the Jewish community, but the problem is essentially the same in both, for the sanction here appealed to is the same. Dr. Judah L. Magnes, president of the Hebrew University in Jerusalem, was long a prominent member of the uncompromising pacifist group in this country. Soon after the Great War he advised that only those be admitted to membership in a pacifist movement who had stood firmly against the war when it came. Today he finds himself sanctioning the Allied cause. But he has no heart for it. "When I support this war," he says, "as unhappily I do, I know that thus I am in conscious rebellion against the divine command. I have not the steadfastness, as once I thought I had, to fulfill this divine command under any and all circumstances. It is a terrible thing to realize that what one thought was part of one's religion is subject to change because of what a single man can do. God has hidden his face from us. We must throw ourselves in the dust and try to find forgiveness. We are transgressing his word knowingly, consciously. We do not know what else to do."[4] It seems to me I have never read a more tragic utterance than this. It is a cry of moral despair—the cry of a soul lost in the search for a sanction for something that he feels must be done whether he finds the sanction or not.

Upon so fine a demonstration of spiritual humility one is reluctant to comment at all. Yet I am constrained to say that the bafflement which these melancholy words reveal is the result of holding a theology which is inherently dualistic. Good and evil are seen as at opposite poles and they completely exclude each other. God is therefore found only in absolute values. He cannot be brought into "profane" history. Hence, if one accepts responsibility for moral living in an evil world with the compromises it entails, he parts company with God. This sounds imaginatively crude, but it is the logical abyss that confronts the person who undertakes to find religious sanctions only in absolute ethical judgments. As I have tried to show earlier, this is a false construction of the meaning of absolutes. To act always in the awareness that the will of God is only partly fulfilled in any practical ethical action is one thing, but to lose the sense of a religious sanction

[4] *Christian Century,* Vol. LVII, March 27, 1940, p. 406.

when making what one regards as a necessary compromise with the brute facts of existence is quite another. Again we need to remind ourselves of an "absolute duty to do our relative best." A valid Christian nurture convinces us that we should always act as under the guidance of God. To choose, when one must, the lesser of two evils is to choose a positive good, and God is presiding over that choice. If a Christian feels called on to fight for his country—if the pacifist alternative is not acceptable to him—he has every right to claim a divine sanction for his act. Any other course will make him a spiritual orphan in a world of reality. Nothing could be more disastrous than to be forced into this ethical "no man's land."

To write this way is of course to invite the most scathing criticism. One is sure to be reproached with having put Jesus on the battlefield. What I am actually saying is that the Christian who is impelled by a valid sense of duty to fight is really, as he believes, finding Christ on the battlefield and joining him there. If Christ has no place on the battlefield, neither has he. The Christian conscience is obligated to take with vast seriousness the question, what would Jesus do? but it is highly important that the answer be given in ethical terms and not merely in terms of sentiment. The Christian finds Christ wherever his conscience bids him go. To hold that the availability of divine sanction is dependent on an infallible judgment of right and wrong is moral defeatism of the most hopeless sort.

I realize the force in what some pacifist Christians are saying on this point. They would prefer that a man disclaim all Christian sanction when he goes to war in order that the strain on his conscience may keep him from the sin of hypocrisy. But this position can be defended, I think, only on the assumption that all participation by Christians in war *is* hypocrisy. Otherwise it is a begging of the question. It is equivalent to saying, "If a man is going to sin, let him do it as a sinner!" The whole question is whether or not there is a valid obligation on the part of a Christian as a citizen to fight. If there is, it is confusion worse confounded to say that he has an obligation to commit a sin. Let him be a conscientious objector and be done with it, or adopt an equally robust ethic that will cover all his obligations. He who finds a Christian sanction for going to war finds it in the sterner aspect of Jesus' ethical teaching as applied to the restraint of wanton violence.

Certain theologians have sought a way out of this dilemma by arguing that although war is always an evil and hence can not result in any positive working of the divine will, nevertheless it may be *negatively* effective by removing obstacles to the doing of that will. For example, if Nazism is thwarting the will of God in the world the Christian may oppose it with force on this purely negative ground. If such reasoning brings comfort to a harassed conscience there may be something to be said for it, but I cannot avoid the feeling that it is naïve and not without danger. The person or the nation that embarks upon so terrible an adventure as modern war can ill afford to take a holiday from all amenability to positive spiritual sanctions. If a Christian is satisfied that war cannot be engaged in with the blessing of God he has no legitimate alternative but to be a conscientious objector. And, by the same token, the Christian community cannot consistently grant to its members the right to fight unless it accepts the principle that, in the particular situation in which the decision has to be made, participation in war has divine sanction.

To say this doubtless invites the charge that the writer is justifying war as a holy crusade. I think this is an unwarranted and confusing assertion. The argument here offered has nothing to do with the concept of a "holy war" in the current sense of that term. The peril in the idea of a "holy war" is that it leads to a complete identification of those who engage in it with the purpose of God in the world. It fosters the assumption that one nation can be the exclusive custodian of that purpose. But this danger is always present in resolute ethical action. The situation confronted in war is not different in kind from that resulting from a domestic political contest in which great values are believed to be at stake. A Christian citizen should not even cast his vote without satisfying himself that he is acting under a high Christian sanction. But if in doing so he identifies the objectives of his party with the Kingdom of God he has become the victim of a costly illusion. The idea of a "holy war" in the sense of a crusade of incorruptible motive and self-justifying purpose is an absurd illustration of the notion of infallible guidance in human affairs. To act ethically in a particular situation requires that one maintain a perspective on life values which quite transcends that situation, and that he subject every act to criticism in the light of consequences that may be reasonably anticipated. But to say that every Christian who declares his belief that in fighting for his country he is doing the will of God is thereby embarking upon a "holy war" is hopelessly to confuse absolute with relative ethical judgments. For the Christian, God is present in the relative as well as in the absolute moral judgment. There are absolute judgments, as there are relative judgments. An example of the former is the judgment that a Christian must always act as a citizen of the Kingdom of God as it is given him to see what such action entails. An example of the latter is the particular judgment that a specified act is in line with the purposes of the Kingdom. Such a judgment is fallible because intelligence is limited, but when supported by all the wisdom one has the sanction for it is complete.

I have perhaps labored this point, but it seems to me one of prime importance. The Christian community is weakened by the equivocal character of its testimony on war, which now tends to condemn many of its members to an "ethical blackout." Condemnation of war as an unmitigated evil requires that the religious body issuing it shall maintain a corporate discipline which forbids participation in war. The pacifist religious groups here act consistently. But if a church is not prepared to support such a discipline it should maintain a full religious sanction for the conscientious participant as it does for the conscientious objector. It may be that the first course, which some of the smaller religious bodies have followed, is the more valid because more in accord with Christian ideals. This is not the question. The Church, broadly speaking, is an institution which has its roots in the world and, again broadly speaking, its members hold themselves responsible for the consequences of action in the political sphere. They live in a precarious world of relative judgments. They do not feel the compulsion of the pacifist vocation. The Christian community to which they belong should not leave them without a spiritual sanction when they are conscientiously impelled toward the bitter alternative of participation in war.

The position here taken may be condemned by many Christians as the exaltation of political loyalty above religious loyalties. That will be a total misconstruction of it. No Christian may ever go to war solely because the State commands it. Conscientious objection to war service is not a prerogative of pacifism, in the absolutist sense of that word. It is always present as an alternative when a Christian is called on to make the decision whether or not to engage in a particular war. If the behest of the State is not in accord with Christian sanctions as the individual sees the matter, the duty to refuse service is plain. The Macintosh case made this issue clear. Dr. Macintosh refused to surrender his judgment as a Christian by unconditional compliance in advance with the State's decree. His was not a pacifist decision, but it was a Christian decision. To do anything different would have been to enthrone the State above the authority of conscience. It is a blot upon our government that the court decision in that celebrated case should have gone all this time unreversed in spite of the stern pronouncement of Mr. Chief Justice Hughes in his memorable dissenting opinion. What I am inveighing against is the failure of the Protestant churches to deal realistically with the war question in ethical terms: either to adopt a thoroughgoing pacifist discipline or to formulate corporate sanctions that will aid their members in deciding under what conditions a Christian may engage in war. Failure to do so perpetuates an ethical dualism, in which the State becomes the custodian of the conscience of the average Christian in wartime. It was this dualism to which Karl Barth referred in his statement concerning Niemöller, quoted in an earlier chapter. When the Church forsakes a man the State takes him up. This ethical failure on the part of the Church actually contributes, I believe, to the continuance of warfare in the world. In an emergency, lacking any corporate testimony that meets the situation, the Church abdicates in favor of the State, instead of being a critic of the State. A few of its members become objectors; the rest follow the flag regardless of where it goes, because they have never been taught to weigh the issue of war under definite sanctions which it is the business of the Christian community to formulate.

It is important to remember that this clarification of Christian moral judgments concerning war is not a simple matter of assessing war guilt. Such a conception of it is not only confusing; it is a perversion of Christian ethics. The making of broad ethical judgments has always for a background the appraisal of forces which are in a significant sense impersonal. They are impersonal to the degree that they have gained a momentum in history which individuals are power-less to stand against. In a given situation, a group, a social class or a nation may be the agency of an evil force which they had nothing to do with originating. This is one of the deep tragedies of history. The decision as to how such forces shall be dealt with has to be made in the face of alternatives that are widely divergent. The possibility of nonviolent resistance is always present to the sensitive Christian mind. But the decision as to which party to a conflict is in the largest measure the agency of evil must be made without reference to "blame." It is not the Christian's business to assess guilt. The Christian view of man does not make him a moral judge over his fellows. "Judge not, that ye be not judged." No ethical obligation resting upon the Christian conscience is more inescapable or more difficult to discharge than the obligation to appraise social forces relentlessly while at the same time withholding condemnation of the human being caught in the web of those forces.

I am aware that philosophical objections may be offered at this point. How can there be social "forces" independent of the conscious choices of individuals? What I am affirming is that just as psychologists recognize the existence of "compulsive" behaviors in individuals—behaviors that result from drives which are not subordinated to rational control—so among social groups and classes, and particularly among nations, there are compulsive collective behaviors in which voluntary choice is reduced to a minimum. This is why it is so often said that the nations of Europe have been marching toward war in spite of a passionate desire on the part of their peoples to preserve peace. Even a people whose government is pronounced an aggressor by the common judgment of mankind and who support that government with their lives may feel a deep devotion to peace.

More reflection upon this aspect of the war question would, I believe, have led to more consistent action by Christians in the matter of economic measures directed against a nation that resorts to aggressive war. Objection to such effort has been offered on the ground that all nations had been equally "guilty." My contention is that this is irrelevant. A father who undertook to reprove his son would be self-condemned if he invoked such a principle. The memory of his own youthful escapades would rise up and choke him. Moral reproof does not involve the imputation of guilt; nor are measures taken to implement that reproof punitive measures. This is the evident meaning of Jesus' words: "Let him that is without sin cast the first stone." The implementation of Christian moral judgments must be remedial, not retributive. And it is precisely the consciousness that we ourselves share in the common guilt for those collective wrongs that are at the root of war that makes it possible to divorce corrective measures from punitive intentions. The pacifist's insistence that the use of coercion always breeds punitive intention is a sobering challenge. But it applies to every use of social coercion, and nowhere more pertinently than in the restraint of criminality within a community. It only serves to emphasize the heroic quality in the Christian ethic. The preservation of social order always necessitates the use of coercion, but in a Christian social order it would be remedial and redemptive, not punitive.

I think this distinction in the realm of motive is the key to the seemingly contradictory teachings of Mahatma Gandhi. He sees no ethical utility in violence as an implementation of hostile attitudes, but he has been outspoken in condemning nonresistance to aggressive cruelty when directed toward others. The duty to defend the helpless takes precedence over the principle of nonresistance. Consider his verbal castigation of the villagers who offered no resistance when their homes were looted by police: "Though I have preached the method of non-violence, I have never desired that the people of India should be helpless cowards and should look on whilst their women are molested. But what did I see this morning? How did the people meet those who looted their houses and molested their women? They showed them their backs. Is this Satyagraha? You may voluntarily allow your property to be looted, and you may bravely face the lathis' blows of the police; you will be then called Satyagrahis, brave men. But rather than look on whilst your women are dishonoured, you should offer physical resistance to them. . . . *Dharma* never teaches cowardice and supine submission to tyranny; *Dharma* teaches us to meet the oppressor bravely and defy him to do his worst. That is the highest law. But *dharma* does not mean flying away from injustice and oppression. . . . If you cannot show the highest heroism, you can certainly show that you are not cowards by dealing a blow for a blow. . . . But you must understand me properly. I do not ask you to be ready to strike on all occasions. If you confront with *lathi* a policeman who comes with a summons or warrant, you are not brave but cowardly. It is no bravery on the part of a crowd of 50 to overwhelm one policeman. You may use force only when the police breaks into your houses, loots your property and threatens the honour of your women."[5]

This statement has no reference to war, but it illuminates the basic issue in the use of physical force. Not the authority of Gandhi's opinion, which is the opinion of one outside the Christian community, but the quality of his analysis is what I would draw attention to.

[5] *Harijan,* Vol. V, No. 50, January 29, 1938, pp. 434-435.

He appeals to force as an impersonal corrective and preventive of evil, not as a vindication of the ethical superiority of those who resort to it.

One important phase of the problem of war in terms of the Christian ethic is not covered in what has been said thus far in this discussion. That is the relation of the Church as a corporate body to the conduct of war. I think there is much to be said for the proposition that even a church which does not maintain a pacifist discipline is obligated to refrain from "blessing" war. I have said that no Christian can consistently engage in armed conflict unless he is convinced that he has the blessing of God in so doing. It does not follow, however, that a church whose membership may be committed to participation in war is warranted in making success at arms the subject of its prayers or in making the maintenance of wartime morale the purpose of its activities and of preachments from its pulpits. The reason for this distinction is that it is gravely doubtful if the mood of corporate repentance and the devotion to redemptive purpose can be preserved in wartime unless the house of worship is totally excluded from the war zone. The task of preserving in wartime the redemptive spirit which is personified in Christ and which is the heart of the Christian ethic is all but impossible. It will be only partially achieved at best. Can we hope for any preservation of Christian motive in an adventure so morally perilous as war inevitably is unless the shrine of the God of Nations is kept inviolate? If the Christian community sanctions participation in war by its individual members the only justification is a faith that throughout the struggle devotion to the universal Christian ideal may be kept alive. If the Church is to "be the Church" in wartime, there will always be kneeling at its altar unseen worshipers who in the flesh are marching under an alien flag but who in the spirit give allegiance to the *Una Sancta*. This is what it means to be the Ecumenical Church.

Chapter VII

DEMOCRACY AND THE
CHRISTIAN ETHIC

IN APPARENT contrast to the picture drawn earlier of a secular culture is the close identification of Christianity with what we regard as our major national ideal—democracy. There has been a marked tendency in liberal Christianity to identify the Christian ethic with the democratic ideal, which is commonly taken as defining the genius of American life and the goal of American education. On closer inspection, however, the relationship between Christianity and democracy is seen to have remained pretty largely in the realm of abstraction. The popular conception of democracy has not risen to the spiritual level. The average American, if asked what democracy means, would doubtless reply, "majority rule." A partly correct answer, of course, but one that refers only to a mechanism which democracy employs. Mr. Lippmann has correctly said, "The justification of majority rule in politics is not to be found in its ethical superiority. It is to be found in the sheer necessity of finding a place in civilized society for the force which resides in the weight of numbers."[1] While democracy of necessity guarantees decision by majority, there is nothing in majority rule that guarantees democracy. And by this I do not mean merely that majorities are often manipulated by minority interests, which is notoriously true, but rather that a *bona fide* numerical majority may and often does, in its treatment of minorities, do grievous violence to democracy, conceived as an ethical principle. For so conceived democracy is a way of life governed by a respect for the dignity of man. My initial contention in this chapter is that we have not yet appropriated in American life such an ethical ideal. Such democracy as we have—and it is by no means to be disparaged—rests upon a secular philosophy, in the sense in which the word "secular" was used in an earlier chapter.

In part, to be sure, democracy expresses an insight of the Founding Fathers into the worth of the common man but, broadly speaking, it has developed as a concomitant of modern economic liberalism and rests on no adequate spiritual foundation. The philosophy underlying it is that of *laissez faire*, a highly individualistic philosophy which sanctions competitive struggle and favors the strong and the fortunate. Politics in an industrial society is an adjunct of economic life. The

[1] *The Phantom Public*, Harcourt, Brace and Company, p. 58.

old term for economics in the curriculum was "political economy," and central in that discipline was the concept of the "economic man." Wherever traditional economics is taught or adhered to that concept remains. It is quite as materialistic a conception as the "economic determinism" of Marxism, but not so frankly espoused as such. The practical difference between the Marxist economics and that believed in by the business community is in the way in which the economic determinant is assumed to work and the outcome that is envisaged. The traditionalist believes that the free play of purely economic forces—the "mechanisms of the market"—will result in an optimum social development, while the Marxist sees in this process inevitable failure and ultimate collapse.

A recent interpreter of totalitarian movements in Europe has brilliantly shown how both these conceptions of social organization have broken down in the Old World. Peter Drucker, in *The End of Economic Man*, presents the thesis that the concept of the "economic man" which underlies both the capitalist system of society and the socialist reconstruction has become bankrupt and that this outmoding of a basic assumption underlying modern civilization is what the fascist revolutions have documented in such melancholy fashion. The strength of those movements lies in their irrationalism—"nihilism," to use Rauschning's term.

First, the prevailing capitalist philosophy was undermined by the failure of "economic man" to produce the good life; then came disillusionment with the Marxist alternative, when it too was seen to depend on exploitive power. Christianity, Mr. Drucker points out, has always opposed the false doctrine of the "economic man." The churches alone among representative social institutions are not built upon economic values. It is the religious forces today that "make life tolerable for the masses" because they are "not exclusively built upon the collapsed concept of economic man." The churches are thus, paradoxically, both stronger than ever and peculiarly impotent. They are "unable to formulate the new constructive concept of society which they pretend to have. Their impotence therefore abets totalitarian fascism, though they should know and actually do know that totalitarianism is far more antireligious and far more opposed to the fundamental beliefs of Christianity than Marxism at its atheistic worst."[2]

Now, we in America have been undergoing on a lesser scale this disillusionment. The inadequacy of the laissez-faire system has become more and more apparent. The reason for this is now widely admitted. The breakdown is an ethical breakdown, but not in the loose and undiscriminating sense in which this

[2] John Day Company, page 100.

is often asserted. Many would have us believe that it is the discipline of hard work that has been neglected, and that the working class is chiefly at fault. But this is to become preoccupied with a symptom and a consequence rather than a cause. The failure in the economic system has been at the point of ethical motive, as current analyses show. Close scrutiny of this failure will reveal, I think, what has been lacking in our conception of democracy as a way of life.

It was a central assumption of the traditional economics that human needs would be met by the automatic working of price. If the production of goods was inadequate, demand would press upward on supply through the stimulus of rising prices; if there should be an excess of supply in relation to effective demand, the imbalance would be automatically corrected as prices fell through the lessened support of demand. It will be noted that the assumption here is that human need will be the determining factor. There is nothing brutal in the theory: self-interest was relied on as a mechanism that would keep prices at the point where a maximum of needed goods would move to market. But what happened showed this elaborate calculation at fault. There grew up the practice of "administering price"—that is, holding price at a given point regardless of the effect on demand and the consequent reduction of output. This practice, while associated with monopoly, has no necessary relation to it. It is rather an economic pattern which industry has evolved in order to minimize risk in times of business uncertainty and instability. It obviates the danger of an unmarketable surplus by restricting production. It involves loss, of course, through the shutdown or curtailed operation of plants, but the prevailing mood of investors and managers has favored acceptance of the loss as against the risk of producing at lower prices in the hope that the stimulated demand will compensate for the lower margin on unit transactions. This means that the immediate interest of the investor, rather than the measure of actual human need becomes the regulatory factor. Thus the classic economic theory, which assumes the dominance of consumer interest in determining the amount of production, has broken down in practice.

It should be noted that the much criticized "plowing under" of crops and destruction of livestock carried out by the New Deal was in reality a drastic application of this well-established economic policy of limiting production in accord with market demand in times of business uncertainty. It was really a concession to the prevailing method of dealing with surpluses in order to sustain prices. Secretary Wallace has gone on record with reference to that method in rather vigorous language. "I confess," he says, "I have always had mingled feelings about this plow-up campaign. It was an amazing demonstration of what a united people can do because they know there is no acceptable alternative. In company with the monetary policy and other measures, it did succeed, to be sure, in raising the farm value of the cotton crop from 464 million dollars in 1932 to 851 million dollars, including AAA payments, in 1933, with immediate results not only on the farm but in increased business in village and city not only down South but elsewhere. We have a trunkful of documentary evidence on that. Nevertheless, to have to destroy a growing crop is a shocking commentary on our civilization. I could tolerate it only as a cleaning up of the wreckage from the old days of unbalanced production. Certainly none of us ever want to go through a plow-up campaign again, no matter how successful a price-raising method it proved to be."[3]

The Brookings Institution, in a number of important studies, has been seeking to convince the business community that this "producer economics" with its defensive strategy is self-defeating. It has assembled evidence that a price policy which takes its start from consumer demand and aims at maximizing production is in the long run sounder and more rewarding.[4]

The central difficulty thus appears to be in a failure to take the long view, and that is always an ethical

[3] *New Frontiers*, Reynal and Hitchcock, pp. 174-175.
[4] See particularly *Industrial Price Policies and Economic Progress*.

failure. Its consequences are accentuated by the fact that the economic system is so tightly geared to the profit motive as to pile up capital accumulations faster than the increase in the buying power of the population on whose demand industry depends. Hence the recurring downward swing into depression. The whole subject is, of course, too complicated to admit of brief discussion. The purpose of this excursion into it is to indicate the collapse of the philosophy of economic liberalism to which democracy has been so closely linked. At this moment democracy in America is lacking any firm philosophic support.

For an epitome of democracy as an ethical ideal we turn naturally to the French Revolution with its slogan: Liberty, Equality, Fraternity. Analysis of these concepts is instructive from the viewpoint of Christian ethics, and indicates the ultimate dependence of democracy upon religion.

Liberty expresses the urge toward personal autonomy. It is something that belongs to man as man and defines in part the noble humanism which is implicit in Christianity but which the philosophy of liberalism has so imperfectly defined. It is, in its elemental form, an expansive, assertive concept. It is a claim upon life as an individual possession. It is a creative urge to break all bonds that limit the powers of the self. It defies exploitation and dooms all tyrannies. When the passion for freedom wanes life goes into eclipse.

Equality, on the other hand, is an ethical mandate to respect the liberty of one's fellows. It is a restrictive, a disciplinary concept. It limits and refines man's elemental demand for liberty, conceived as absence of external restraint. It is a personalizing principle, bringing the individual into that harmony with his fellows which an organic society requires. Thus liberty and equality are antithetic concepts in that the concern for equality can be implemented only by curtailing the liberty of those who enjoy either superior endowments or superior advantage. The two ideals are in a very definite sense at war with each other. Liberty pursued as an individual end makes for a class society, negating the classlessness that equality implies. Without an integrating principle there could be no resolution of this conflict.[5]

Fraternity, the third term of the trinitarian formula of democracy, furnishes this integrating principle. If we think of liberty and equality in dialectical terms as opposites that tend to interpenetrate, fraternity becomes the synthesis in which the meaning of the other two terms is finally explicit. Thus equality is seen as the complement of liberty. Its recognition is the cumula-

[5] Dean William F. Russell has developed this idea in interesting fashion in his little book, *Liberty vs. Equality,* Macmillan Company.

tive effect of unsatisfied demands on the part of the less advantaged majority to participate in those goods of life which the few are able to possess by a liberty that is unrestrained. It was a true insight of the pioneers of the modern democratic movement that its purpose could never be realized except as men were influenced by a sentiment of fraternity—active good will among men as members of a community.

Reverting to our theological discussion we may regard equality as one of the great religious myths. It has no factual reference. It is a spiritual affirmation that every person has equal claim with every person to a chance to be all that it is in him to be. Such an affirmation can be validated only in personal living motivated by active good will, which is what fraternity means. It is at this point that the tremendous relevance of Christianity to the democratic ideal becomes evident. It furnishes a deeper insight than that of the French revolutionaries—that fraternity can be experienced only as man sees in his fellow the *Imago Dei*, the authentic imprint of the finger of God. If the French Revolution was to a great extent abortive, may that result not be due to the failure to find for the ideal of fraternity this ultimate ground in universal Spirit?

In the light of such considerations the contemporary discussion of democracy in America seems thin and unreal. We are admonished by representatives of business and industry to come to the defense of free economic enterprise since that is indispensable to the preservation of political and religious liberty. We are reminded that in Germany free economic enterprise was tampered with—and look at the result. Russia likewise. This is plausible; it is sincere; in a measure it is no doubt true. But it comes at the truth backwards, and invites the wrong inferences. The peril in which democracy finds itself is due in great part to the failure of the economic system to furnish a material basis upon which democracy might rest. For democracy is not a concomitant of economic enterprise. It is a prior principle, which economic enterprise must serve or collapse under the pressure of insistent humanity. Little by little—though sometimes with startling suddenness—mankind is learning that the essential divinity of man is a "first principle," not a derivative. Every system for the ordering of human affairs must justify itself by reference to that principle. It has been said that it makes all the difference in the world "whether truth is put in the first place or in the second place." If put in the second place it can not be "put" at all. Neither can democracy. It is not a device. It is not a by-product. It is the foundation on which the durable organization of human life must rest.

The evidence that we in America have not taken democracy seriously is grievously abundant. Most conspicuously it appears in the status inflicted upon our colored population. Now, merely to mention this question is, I venture to say, to start the reader's minds working on the so-called Negro problem! Why is there a Negro problem? *Where* is the Negro problem? It is in the hearts of the white people. It becomes a social problem only because of stubborn attitudes in human beings who are on the privileged side of the color line. What I mean is that color in itself is a neutral quality in human beings until it is made the badge of status. Black, in this country, stands for an inheritance of bondage. It is the hallmark by which the white population is reminded of its great collective sin in enslaving human beings. And men habitually visit their own sins against their fellows upon their victims. We tend to love least those we have wronged. By maintaining the fiction of race or group inferiority we rationalize conduct that implies such inferiority.

All this has nothing to do with the scientific question of race differences. I am aware that merely citing the testimony of anthropologists to the effect that race inferiority is fictional has little influence upon deep-seated emotional attitudes. Even if it were assumed that a differential in intelligence exists to the advantage of the white "race," that difference would be inconsiderable as compared with measured differences among whites within the same social club, the same church, even the same family. No, the question is not one for the scientist—save as human attitudes create problems for the sociologist. The "problem" is ethical. Jesus would know precisely where to locate it.

My contention is that this Number One ethical issue in American democracy can be settled only by a spiritual achievement on the part of the white population: learning to regard the Negro as primarily a person and incidentally a colored man. This would mean that as a mere matter of broad human justice he be emancipated from the corporate disabilities now imposed upon him. No one disputes the fact that cultural levels have a bearing on human relationships. Ignorance is measurably a bar to social intercourse. Poverty and disease stand in the way of brotherhood as a realized experience. What the white population has done to the Negro is to keep him on an economic and cultural level that prevents him from participating in the cultural heritage of the nation, and then to justify that course by pointing to the results of its own act! We commit this sin through flagrant violation of Constitutional rights in the matter of voting, through inhuman discrimination in the use of school funds, and even through exclusion from trade-union membership. Then we talk about the race question defensively—as if the Negro, once accorded his place in the sun, would consider it a prize to further adulterate the blood of his race! The bogey of social equality (always interpreted in terms of miscegenation) is, I believe, kept alive chiefly by the enforcement upon the colored people of an economic and political inferiority which has no relation to native capacity.

This question of race is the number one ethical issue not only of the nation but also of the Church. In vain do we proclaim in the familiar ecumenical terms that the Church is "supra-race" so long as it takes over without protest or criticism the social pattern of segregation. I am fully aware that this custom cannot be eradicated at a stroke. All through these lectures we have recognized the difference between the absolute ethic of Jesus and its inevitably gradual implementation in our common life. It is characteristic of the Christian ethic that it maintains a tension between man even at his best and that perfection which for the Christian community is represented by Jesus Christ. And the Church rightly fosters the mood of repentance on the part of men and women who, on their highest levels of conduct, are still "unprofitable servants." All this flows inevitably from the recognition of an absolute ethic without which religion would have lost its prophetic quality. But the boundary between confession and hypocrisy is perilously narrow. The salvation of an unprofitable servant is attained only as he becomes less unprofitable. The church or the religious organization that accepts race segregation in humility and pain because of outward social pressures may claim to be "in the Way"; but when it ceases to feel the scandal of the Cross it has lost the Way. The Church is by its very nature the institution which should carry primary responsibility for democratizing race relations. If men cannot meet at the altar of God, where else shall they meet?

The basic problem of economic democracy in America has already been indicated in recording the collapse of the philosophy of liberalism upon which democracy has depended for theoretical support. Partisan political issues we are not here concerned with, but it is highly in order to point out that the strength which the New Deal has been able to muster at the polls is irresistible testimony to the primary importance of the issues with which it has persistently concerned itself. I have never been able to see anything very convincing in the contention that the masses have been so seduced by Santa Claus that no valid political judgments may be expected from them at the polls. Now, to the extent that the administration of relief has been corrupted for political ends the argument is one hundred per cent sound. The best that can be said for such administration is what Mr. Lippmann has said: that so long as there is a huge relief problem there will be politics in relief. But this offers no shadow of excuse for political manipulation of relief funds. Corruption remains corruption no matter how many explanations can be offered for it. But my point is that the Santa Claus argument attacks the problem at the wrong end. As stated, it would seem to be an argument against the human race. The human fondness for Santa Claus is pretty well and honorably established. Some very beautiful and rewarding experiences in all our lives have been based upon it. But that the average American workingman prefers a public Santa Claus to a private pay envelope is a proposition that I find hard to accept. The brute fact is the long-continued existence of human need and insecurity throughout the nation. The statistics are so well known that to record them here would be gratuitous. All argument over whose fault unemployment is is beside the point—and grossly misleading. It is a collective fault, because it involves national policy, and is not to be placed on the doorstep of any one individual, party or group. That is why the condition is so persistent and so baffling. This much, at least, can be confidently said: there will be no domestic peace, no national unity, until the common man is given a chance to earn a respectable livelihood, and if this is not done by enlightened voluntary action on the part of those who own and control economic enterprise it will perforce be done by government.

This brings us to the all-important question of the

economic function of the State. It must, I think, be admitted that the centralization in government of control over economic life involves great dangers. Not only does it increase the likelihood of political abuses but it blurs an important distinction between political and nonpolitical functions. As society becomes more and more complex the things that matter in human affairs require specific forms of organization with decentralized control. The more centralization we have, the less real functional control can we expect. The life-sustaining and the life-enriching functions are so many and diverse that they cannot profitably be centrally administered, nor can the necessary decisions be made in wholesale fashion. The wholesome growth of democracy is marked by the assumption of control by functional groups, under appropriate state and federal supervision, of economic processes. Certainly it is easier at this moment to envisage the attainment of democratic ends by such means than by a continued extension of government control. The larger and more responsible the State becomes the more desirable it is that its control over specialized functions be potential rather than actual, supervisory rather than detailed.

The basis of the distinction just suggested between political and nonpolitical functions is to be found in the existence of two distinct sets of interests on the part of every citizen. He is a member of a community

living in a particular locality, and as such he shares
with all other residents in the community certain common needs. Among them, are protection of his person
and his domicile, provision for the education of his
children, facilities for buying what he needs, recrea-
tion, cultural opportunities, and similar requirements.
All these are needs that are wholly independent of his
economic status as producer—the way he makes his
living. Economically speaking, they concern him rather
as consumer. These needs are shared throughout a community, some of them limited to the local community,
some concerning the state, and some the nation. They
may therefore be characterized as territorial, rather
than functional. This same person, as producer,
whether of goods or services, has interests in common
with all those in his trade or profession no matter
where they live. These interests may be called functional, as distinguished from territorial. Now the territorial control of society is the primary sphere of politics.
That is to say, it concerns all the people living in a given
area, which for purposes of such control is constituted
a political unit. In this unit some measure of political
sovereignty inheres. No one but an anarchist would
dispense with political power in this sense of territorial
control. In the functional area of life, however, control,
in a democratic regime, inheres in voluntarily constituted groups and as such is nonpolitical in nature. To

be sure, we speak of labor politics, school politics and church politics, but such terms are strictly metaphorical. In these functional areas, the State in a society like ours has no original jurisdiction, if we may so use the term. The State is always potentially present, since no functional interest may be allowed to encroach upon the total community's interest. Also the State must defend one individual or group from injury by another. But this is in the nature of police power and is invoked only when the "public" is considered to have an important stake in what is happening. An industry, for example, may not infringe the rights of the individual with respect to health. There is a metaphysical principle underlying all this: the State is conceived as existing in the person of its nationals and suffering injury whenever they are injured.

Now the boundary between these spheres of action—political and nonpolitical—is never sharply fixed. An important zone of conflict is that of "civil liberty" in which the immunities of a person as citizen are continually requiring definition and protection in communities that are dominated by powerful industries. Again, the controversy over economic planning focuses on the boundary between State action and voluntary action with reference to the control of business and industrial enterprise. In terms of the foregoing analysis this means that the interest of people as consumers (territorial) are continually becoming paramount—as in the case of unemployment or inadequate income—and so causing the political sphere to press in upon the economic.

Experience seems to show that society as a whole has much at stake in the functional principle, that is, in centering responsibility in the functional group. Broadly speaking, political power is ill-adapted to the control of special functions except those that belong in the territorial sphere. This applies also to a wide range of functions other than economic. The separation of Church and State is a recognition of this principle. The distinguishing characteristic of extra-political functions is their voluntary quality. For while the State is not to be regarded, in a democracy, as an instrument of arbitrary force, it is nevertheless distinguished from all other institutions by its ultimate right, so far as human authority goes, to use force. Hence the basic ethical problem of political democracy is the problem of power. Christianity has thus far addressed itself to the opposition to power (in its contest with the State) and to the dissemination of power (in its support of political democracy). It has still to address itself to the purification of power through the application to it of the principle of vocation. As Mounier says, speaking of the exercise of political power by a Christian, "Authority . . . taken politically, is a vocation which the person receives from God . . . The duty which authority has of serving persons predominates over any powers which positive law may grant to its functions. It is essentially a vocation to rouse other persons."[6] This means that Lord Acton's much quoted statement is only partly true. "Power," he said, "always corrupts, and absolute power corrupts absolutely." The latter part of this statement is so true and so terribly important that it affords a license to quote the first part, but in the view here taken the first part is not true. "Power," says Max Lerner, "is what you make it." The ethical responsibility of the State is to denature power of the arbitrary and insidious quality to which Lord Acton referred by making it the authentic instrument of the community. In a very real sense, what was said in an earlier chapter about the nature of prophecy applies to the nature of political power.[7] There we said that a prophetic pulpit affords no private prerogatives; that the minister, as preacher, must continually seek to render judgments that flow so inevitably from the commonly accepted Christian testimony that even those who dislike to hear his words will recognize their authentic quality. Now a government attempting to function under a majority mandate is nevertheless the government of the whole people. The acid test of its

[6] *Op. cit.*, pp. 247-248.
[7] See Chapter IV.

administration is the justice done to minorities. This is beautifully illustrated in theory in the British tradition of "His Majesty's Loyal Opposition." It is "His Majesty's" and it is "loyal." In a democracy, a person belonging to a political minority must, of course, acquiesce in policies to which he is opposed. But in a true democracy he will, as a citizen, have the same equity in the government as if his party were in power and he will therefore feel more truly represented as a citizen *because the majority will is being executed* than if his own minority party had by some chance managed to get control of the government. There is this much of validity in Rousseau's theory of the Social Contract. When the common will is being done in authentic fashion the minority does participate by virtue of a wholehearted commitment to the democratic process.

The bearing of the Christian ethic on this problem of power is therefore clear. To the mind of Jesus, power could never be used coercively except as a redemptive act. To use it for private ends would be a profanation. Indeed, spiritual power so diverted would evaporate and leave only impotence in its place. Again, the essence of authority is in vocation.

It seems to me that in the voluntary, functional type of organization we have the most important laboratory of democracy in American life. The Church is one such organization and has its share of responsibility for this process. Not the least important aspect of the relation between Christianity and democracy is the opportunity for a demonstration of democratic action in the government of the Church itself. It is doubtful if, on the whole, the affairs of our churches are any more democratically administered than those of secular agencies. Indeed, in many instances the comparison would be disadvantageous to the Church. Where, for example, in a society composed of both men and women would one find a more man-dominated institution than many of our churches are? And in spite of all gestures toward democratic procedure and the claim that Protestant churches are lay institutions, are not most of them pretty thoroughly under the control of their ministers? (Imagine a Catholic parishioner saying to his friends that he is going to Dr. Blank's church this morning!)

But the relation of the Church to the democratic process is vastly greater than anything that happens within its walls. Protestant emphasis on the lay "calling" is extremely important for our time. It needs to be revived in full strength. In trade or professional association, in labor union, in factory, in school and college—wherever people are busy making a living or making a life, they are confronting one another on the basis of certain assumptions. Whether these relationships are assumed to be an expression of mutual respect, individual self-restraint, voluntary initiative, group thinking and judgment, or the reverse of these attitudes and processes, may determine ultimately how much democracy America is to have. While we are preoccupied with what goes on at Washington or at our state capitals the fate of our democracy may be decided in our schoolhouses, factories, churches and labor unions. Wherever there are co-operative human relations in which men treat each other as ends rather than as means; in which they reason, not intimidate; in which the humblest person carries all the weight that the quality of his thought and conscience justifies; in which every one participates in the decisions by which he is affected; in which men learn to make choices and face the consequences—wherever these qualities of life obtain there is a school of democracy. These qualities have to be achieved in everyday essential activities. They belong to the stuff of the common life. They are communicated "to persons through persons." They sanctify the vocational act and give to all life a sacramental character. In other words they personalize life after the fashion of the personality of Jesus.

In this chapter as in the last we have been trying to uncover a meaning in the Christian social ethic that is not just an application of New Testament precepts to the "social order" but an infusion of Christian motive into elemental relationships—into the culture itself. The burden of much of the criticism directed at the social gospel is its externalism, its preoccupation with structure and mechanics. The social gospel does indeed acquire its distinctive emphasis at the point of application to the structure of the common life—to industry, trade and government. But unless spiritual principles are internalized through face-to-face relationships they remain theories and blueprints and never enter into life. Up to now our ideas of democracy have been largely academic—concerned with long and short ballots, with initiative and referenda, with party discipline and "getting out the vote"—and we have given scant attention to the basis of democracy in family, school, church, shop and business relationships. Democracy is both a vision and a discipline. It sees through all defects and distortions the supremely human—the *Imago Dei*. It orders life so that personal encounters bring out the human best.

A grievous lack in the common conception of democracy and of the ethics of human relationships is the failure to grasp the reciprocal element in the encounter between persons in significant social relationships. We understand mutuality—the sharing of experiences had in common—and grasp without difficulty the spirit of the Golden Rule, which rests on mutuality. The force of the words "as ye would" lies in the fact that we are related to our fellows on a basis of likeness. But many of the most significant human relationships are based on differences—on reciprocality rather than mutuality. Consider, for example, the husband-wife, parent-child, employer-employe relationships. That there is a ground of mutuality, of common humanity, underlying everything here would go without saying. But that which is distinctive in these relationships arises not out of likeness but out of difference. To eradicate this difference, which has a quality of oppositeness, would annihilate the relationship. In lesser degree this is true even of friendship, to which challenging differences give an added charm. My point here, however, is that the conduct of human affairs requires an ordered relationship between persons whose functions in society make them reciprocal to each other. Thus it becomes an advantage to each that every other be and act his distinctive self. Were this not so strife and jealousy between people of differing endowments would be bitter beyond endurance. The singer on the opera stage is not regarded by the listener in the audience with fierce envy because he can sing so well, but with admiration and delight because he can banquet our ears with music which but for his talent we should be without. An ideal society would not be one in which every one treated every one else precisely as he himself would like to be treated. The singer and the listener cannot change places. The partners in reciprocal relations can never change places. The Golden Rule applies literally in all relationships of mutuality but it surely was never intended to be applied literally to relationships the key to which is reciprocality.

This reciprocal quality in the relations of persons rests of course on functional difference. And this difference is of crucial importance in the ethics of democracy. We have said that authority is rightly understood as a vocation—that is, as a function exercised by virtue of one's membership in an organic and functional society. This means that the exercise of power and authority in a democratic setting is a response to need, to social demand, never the unilateral use of an instrument of private advantage. Authority is never legitimately "wielded," but rather, appropriated by those whom authority serves, as social leadership. Equality, as an ethical principle, means a right to whatever resources one needs in order to be his distinctive self, that is to say, in order that society may not be deprived of his distinctive service. This is his true liberty. (Christianity must never be bullied out of using the excellent slogan, "To each according to his need" just because the Communists have made use of it!) And the reciprocal functional character of creative human relationships is the visible sign of fraternity.

The practice of democracy requires therefore the

most extensive facilities for functional interaction. In orderly association in functional groups men develop competence; in reciprocal relations with other functional groups they perfect social processes. This is the ethical warrant for collective bargaining in industry, a principle in the recognition of which we in America have been so tardy. To see in trade-union activity merely the exercise of collective might is to see it only in its crude and degenerate form. Rightly understood, and when properly functioning, a labor union is a social instrument. It has its frankly defensive features, as have all functional organizations, because of the deep-seated assertiveness of human beings, and the peril that lurks in power. But the labor union has its social justification in the functional nature of society which we have been considering. Responsibility can be intelligently and competently exercised only when it is efficiently organized. The professions learned this long ago. The concept of "professional ethics" grows out of such recognition. It is a true insight on the part of the Catholic Church that it regards participation in collective labor action not only as a "right" but as a social duty. This is an inevitable result of extending the concept of democracy from the political to the nonpolitical realm. As an ethical principle it has binding obligations in every sphere where people undertake in orderly fashion to do things together. I look forward to a time when the duty to belong to and participate in functional associations will be on the same footing as the duty to vote. Indeed, the neglect of the techniques of group relationships in business and professional life is largely responsible for our habitual helpless falling back on the power of the State to secure for us what we should be able to secure for ourselves. Voluntary arbitration of trade disputes, which has acquired a considerable vogue, is an excellent example of democratic functioning. Facilities for developing standards of social control with reference to radio, the stage and the screen, for example, through the voluntary collaboration of influential groups having a legitimate interest, would be the best insurance against arbitrary censorship which does so much harm in order to do some good.

In a different way, but quite as significantly, the democratic process is fostered in such activities as characterize the consumers' co-operative movement. Here we are back in the "territorial" type of association, in which people meet as residents of a community rather than on the basis of producer functions. This might be called quasi-political action in that it represents a geographic area, but on the voluntary level. A group approach to the elemental consumer function has been found to be a broadly socializing and educative experience.

Another fruitful basis of organization is parenthood —the experience of rearing children which adult members of a community share. Parent associations organize one of the most basic of human interests and one that has unlimited ramifications in community life.

All this means that in a community which owns allegiance to Christianity those functions and relationships on which life depends should be continually explored and refined in the pursuit of Christian vocation. This is an area in which, in Protestant theory, the Church, as Church, has little direct responsibility. Voluntary functional organizations, on the other hand, of Christian men and women in vocational groups, seeking continually to pervade social life with Christian ethical assumptions may be an influence of great potency. It is, perhaps, in this way that the democratic implications of Christianity can be most effectively implemented in action. The social faith underlying this expectation is the personalist faith that when human beings are seen by one another as embodiments of the divine, all their relationships will be shot through with creative good will.

A basic assumption of democracy is the validity of popular judgment on questions of policy. Woodrow Wilson said he had great faith in the American people "when they are fully informed and free to act." Today much concern is felt over the way in which popular judgment is vitiated by the influence of propaganda. The extent of this concern is evidenced by the wide use of the publications of the Institute for Propaganda Analysis and the many books that have been aimed at unmasking under-cover interests. But the problem is complicated.

The current movement to combat propaganda is highly significant by reason both of its prophylactic value and of its revelation of a new state of mind. The powerful propagandas of special interests, both economic and political, have inevitably brought about a reaction, a sort of immunization of the public mind. This protective tendency has been furthered by the movement for propaganda analysis. It may be that the enormous exploitation for propaganda purposes of all channels of communication has aroused so great a reaction that it must run its rather uncritical course. If so, it will be a demonstration of how great a price society pays for large-scale exploitation. For the tendency to cry, "Propaganda!" when any serious effort is made to influence public opinion, no matter how free from commercial interest, is anything but wholesome. I wonder if in the effort to render the people immune to the propaganda of special interests we are not actually rendering them allergic to all appeals to reason or to moral judgment. If I had to choose between credulity and cynicism, I think I would take the former.

This, however, is only to say that the movement to bring propaganda under control needs to be more fully assimilated to the total educative process. It will then be appreciated that independence of judgment ceases to be a virtue if it divorces a person from the social process by which group attitudes are formed. Also, that wholesome attitudes are not based solely on intellectual judgments but upon loyalties that have a way of sustaining themselves by the fervor they arouse. To foster private judgment on social issues has its dangers. To put it differently, private judgment has definite limitations. Democracy requires "independent" thinking, but not independent in the sense of isolation from what is going on in the minds of others. Here lies the great paradox of democracy. It exalts the individual, but only by giving him deeper roots in the mental and spiritual community of which he is a part.

The terrific urgency in the present world situation makes it all but impossible to steer a straight course in individual thinking or in national policy. We are committed to democracy, yet we have as a nation only an imperfect apprehension of what it means and are still farther from wholehearted commitment to as much democracy as we theoretically accept. We are now halting between two alternatives—to fight (or to be ready to fight) for the preservation of such democracy as we have against the aggression of tyrannical power, or to remain aloof from the struggle in order that this democracy may not degenerate into the thing it opposes. The partisans of these two positions seem too well established in their thinking to be affected by argument. In any case, momentous decisions may have been reached before these lines appear in print. However, some few things seem clear enough to set down.

First, our democracy is worth fighting for, or suffering for, for conscience' sake, only if it is seen as a way of life deriving its authority from the enthronement of personality, from the exaltation of the common man as a child of God, and only if we are determined that America shall progressively realize that ideal. This requires a spiritual imagination and a discipline of life to which few, if any, of us have attained. Even in our schools and our churches we are far from placing that high value upon the individual person which alone justifies the time and labor and patience that the democratic process entails. Nor are we as a people ready to give a decent economic status to that vast portion of our population to whom democracy today is either a tenuous dream or a rather ghastly joke. The simple fact is that democracy cannot be had without sacrificial effort, even though we refuse to go to war in its defense.

Secondly, the decision to maintain aloofness from the war—assuming that it will not actually infringe our independence—will be equivalent to a decision to carry much farther the reconstruction of our domestic economy. Whatever hope conservative minds may have entertained of rehabilitating the laissez-faire economy with its highly individualistic conception of democracy is being dissipated as world trade is drawn into the totalitarian orbit. If we are unable or unwilling to challenge Nazism in the rest of the world, it seems certain that we must subject our economic life to a planning process which will make a self-contained economy possible. If we isolate ourselves from the world we shall either have much more of democracy at home or we shall soon have much less. To contend that we must "preserve" democracy at home by refusing to jeopardize it by waging war is not enough. The peril to democracy that lurks in war is not to be minimized, but complacency about "our American institutions" when so large a part of our people are living in insecurity and frustration involves at least equivalent peril.

Thirdly, should America be drawn into the conflict that with a terrible fatality has engulfed the Old World, we shall be under a heavy moral obligation to subordinate every private interest to the purpose not merely of winning a war but of making the results commensurate with the sacrifice. In a contemplative mood one of America's ablest writers recently penned the following:

> On Memorial Day in 1918, just before I entered the army, I went and sat among the long ranks of little square headstones in the National Cemetery at Arlington, across the Potomac from Washington. I imagined Lincoln in the White House, and these boys, now so long absent from life, still able to see what had happened to the Republic their lives had been ended to save. Had their survivors made the nation into something that was worth what they had given? Partly, perhaps, but not enough, not nearly enough. On a thousand counts they had been betrayed. How could the living be brought to devote as much shivering and sweat and heartiness and pain and courage and hard-headed ingenuity to the future as the dead had done? . . .
>
> . . . A static America, an America that looks backward only, an America that defends what it has, cynically and needlessly endures unemployment and poverty, exploits and debases its science and its art, cannot live. It will be no more able to shelter itself against the vigorous barbarians at home or abroad than have the democracies of Europe under their decadent leadership. For I have a premonition, as do many others, that this war is not primarily a war of nations. Its basic meaning is revolutionary. What we must prepare for is not merely to survive the onslaught of the foreign horde, but to be worthy of survival.[8]

[8] George Soule, "What Are We To Defend?" *The New Republic*, June 10, 1940, p. 782.

I have argued that democracy as a purely secular ideal is bound to be ineffectual—that it requires the support of a spiritual ethic. It is no less true, I believe, that Christianity has arrived at one of its great historical moments, when in order to achieve full relevance to the common life it must render its message explicit in terms of the democratic way of human relationships. To fail in this task would be to deny its own nature.

INDEX

[257]

INDEX

[258]

INDEX

INDEX

INDEX